SE A»

URSULA PERUCCHI-PETRI

CUCCHI

Drawings 1975 - 1989

«LA DISEGNA»

This book first appeared as the catalog for the exhibition:
Enzo Cucchi «La Disegna» - Zeichnungen 1975 bis 1988.
Kunsthaus Zürich (9-9 / 30-10-1988).
Louisiana Museum Humlebaek (12-11-1988 / 5-1-1989) and
Kunstmuseum Düsseldorf (15-1 / 5-3-1989).

Frontispiece: *Ritratto di casa.* Incontri Internazionali d'Arte, Roma, 1977.
Jacket: Enzo Cucchi in Cairo.

First published in the United States of America in 1990 by
RIZZOLI INTERNATIONAL PUBLICATIONS, INC.
300 Park Avenue South, New York, NY 10010

Translation by Richard-Lewis Rees

LC 89-43580
ISBN 0-8478-1203-0

Printed and bound in Spain by La Polígrafa, S. A.
Parets del Vallès (Barcelona)
Dep. Leg. B. 6.695 - 1990

CONTENTS

BETWEEN EARTH AND HEAVEN

In 1982 the Kunsthaus of Zürich presented an exhibition of Enzo Cucchi's large-format drawings. This concentration on his large formats created between 1980 and 1982 made possible the reconstruction of the initial state of Cucchi's studio in the old church of Gallignano. The spacious church premises, which the artist had been using as his place of work since 1980, offered him the opportunity to work with formats of up to 2¾ yards high by 6½ yards wide (2.5 m×6 m), while the drawings themselves complemented each other and maintained a mutual internal relationship. It was not exactly by chance therefore that at this time Cucchi developed the concepts of "saints" and "heroes," of "marvellous landscapes" and "miracles of stone." The atmosphere of the sacred enclosure exercised an unquestionable influence over him, while thanks to the monumentality characteristic of murals, Cucchi discovered new possibilities for drawing.

Since then not only have the artist's works been shown in the most important museums in the world but he has also taken part in a great number of international exhibitions, for which he has normally chosen to group together those works that make up a single family. The aim of this book, however, is to offer for the first time a sufficiently extensive and representative overview of the development of his work, from 1975 until the present day, based on his small format drawings. From the very beginning, these drawings have occupied the center of Cucchi's activities. As he says, they are his soul, and as the foundation of his artistic activity, they provide us with direct insight into the genesis of his imaginist universe. In these he soon reveals themes which later appear in paintings, sculptures, reliefs, and graphic works.

Cucchi's work has undergone profound changes since 1982, among other reasons due to the inclusion into his artistic repertoire of sculpture, which has subsequently come to play a crucial role in his activities as a whole. In this way the artist has clearly moved far away from what at first critics attempted to define as the Transavantgarde. The representatives of this tendency (Chia, Clemente, De Maria, Paladino) had burst in upon the artistic scene at the end of the seventies with an impressive show of creativity. However, after the hegemony of North American art begun in the fifties and a universally sought "internationalism" had both declined, European artists once again started to seek inspiration in their own traditions. Regionalism was no longer equated with provincialism; on the contrary, local "dialects" once again revealed their own inner force.[1] So it is by no means surprising that Cucchi spoke with admiration of Carlo Carrà and De Chirico, as well as of other artists from the thirties, such as Scipione or Sironi, and even of objects such as votive offerings, whose ingenuous popular character Cucchi valued highly. Like the representatives of the "pittura metafisica," he was drawn to the old Italian masters, especially Giotto, Piero della Francesa, and Masaccio, but also to Caravaggio. Alongside the aforementioned painters, over the years figures such as Victor Hugo, Odilon Redon, Alfred Kubin, and Lucio Fontana have also acquired importance for him. Finally, the return to the pictorial works of the Italian tradition is accompanied by the rediscovery of myths understood as spiritual potential with which to surpass an exclusively rationalist cosmovision.

The ups and downs in the life of Enzo Cucchi the man, represented in the iconography of his work and in his texts, seem to affect him more intensely as his own personality develops. If formerly he stated that he never drew for pleasure, now this same statement expresses almost desperation. For Cucchi there is no pleasure to be found in drawing or staying in his studio; he works moved by the responsibility of doing what has to be done. "Spiritual discipline," "heroism," and "energy" are recurrent expressions which define his attitude. His works are infused with a tragic authenticity; for Cucchi, all forms of cynicism are unknown. For him drawing is something existential, linked to ideas of its wide possibilities. One of his first works (1978) already bore the title *Portami a terra in un disegno* (Carry me to Earth in a Drawing), and in his recent text for *Il*

Cannocchiale we read: "The idea of a drawing is the only opportunity for a man to think." For Cucchi the drawing is "the true, existential soul of the painter"; he must never "narrate" or "illustrate" or "describe." Drawing, concentrated in a sign, is for him a "place of mystery and wonder" which keeps his secret. The concept of wonder—"meraviglia"—is of capital importance in the work of Cucchi. It emerges when the drawing becomes necessary; and, to tell the truth, it emerges not only for the artist but also for the observer. It is the extraordinary state of the moment of creation, which later may be conveyed to the observer.

In the catalogue for the 1987 exhibition *Guida al disegno*, Ulrich Weisner tells of a conversation he had with the artist about the concept of "disegno." In the conversation, Cucchi said "In certain cases it's correct to translate it as 'drawing.' But 'disegno' is more than the representation of a thing. The word should also be understood on the conceptual plane. It's true that the artist represents a thing, but at the same time he says something more, and as he wants to transmit something 'between the lines,' the observer must also read 'between the lines.' "[2] For Cucchi drawing is "an idea of the world, the idea of a thing and, in this sense, something unreal." In drawing—says Cucchi during our conversations—a reality is produced and, at the same time, something "incredible emanates from it, something that crosses frontiers." The "sign" bears a relation to "memory." This concept, which is also important for Cucchi, alludes in the first place not to his own memory but to the roots of a very ancient tradition we carry inside us. He understands that once something has existed, it endures for ever. He speaks of "mobile moments between the past and the present which illuminate the future" and of the "verticality" that begins from the floor of history and completes individual experience, a "vision orientated towards the heights."[3] The important thing is "that subterranean flow, that movement through time."[4] Such concepts acquire visual form, for example, in paintings such as his 1984 *Millennial Transport*[5] (see p. 14). Since Cucchi has been spending much of the year in Rome, he has lived constantly surrounded by this tradition born from history. He speaks of his "double level," and says that today it is possible for art to "advance on a double level, advance on the level of reality and on another level." This has nothing to do with anachronism.

Cucchi places his hope on “the sign that carries history inside, which marks, transported by the immensity of things, by peoples....”[6]

In our conversations it becomes clear what “sign” means for Cucchi. A sign must always refer to something: “When Piero della Francesca paints an arm, what he paints is not the description of an arm.” Every image is “an impulse,” “a chariot that advances, a sign in search of another sign.” “Signs that describe are closed, inalterable.” By contrast, a sign that “signs” is open, mysterious: it liberates. This sign “walks, proceeds, charges, discharges, recharges... always the same things.” The act of charging and discharging is none other than the driving force. Here the idea of the “sign” flows into the broad conceptual stream of “transport” and “journey,” which plays such a decisive role in his work (see p. 11).

After my first work experience with Enzo Cucchi's art, the fruit of which was his charcoal drawing exhibition of 1982, his oeuvre has acquired a multiplicity of registers. In 1985, during a debate on the manifesto prepared together with Bruno Corà for the “Solchi d'Europa,” Cucchi spoke about present-day prospects for creating a work of art. The artist continually strives to capture “the totality of things,” to achieve “a vision of the interior.” For this the prime requisite is “a return to sentiments in order once again to have a creative idea.” The vision can take form only on the “basis of sentiments,” “where the material of the work of art, converted into form, must be a mobile material.” In the debate, Bruno Corà and Enzo Cucchi agreed that today it is no longer possible to “speak of the work of art from outside,” and that what must be done is “capture its inner quality and live side-by-side with the work of art.”[7] How can an art historian today write about works in which hardly anything else is visible except “inner visions,” archetypal images, and metaphors? Cucchi's drawings resist unambiguous interpretations, and access to them obviously cannot be gained through the intellect alone. The important thing is that his messages, his “signs,” should awaken in the observer imaginative associations and emotional processes that he will be able to re-elaborate and convert into a new experience. In an attempt to interpret the works of Cucchi, critics have often referred to the myths and legends of his country. However, an in-depth study of his “images” reveals that he hardly ever takes concrete myths or legends as his starting point.

For this reason, our plan to find a means of access to his work by tracing the development of some of his motifs over the years is based on the closest possible approach to his drawings. The fact that we speak only of an approach is due to the very nature of works of art, which acquire plenitude by guarding their secrets.

Transport and Travel

Even in his very first drawings, Cucchi was already dealing with the subject of transport and travel. In one from 1979 we observe that the transport in question is of unusual objects: a coach drawn by a lean horse carries two trees and a house, elements of vital importance for the artist, as we shall see later on. The coachman embraces in his wide open arms a wheel suspended in air which, by virtue of its singular position, is reminiscent of a sun disc or a wheel of life. The objects in the composition sprout from graphic signs and lines of energy that provide the artist with the basis for his inventions. This style, characteristic of his early period, similarly presides over another drawing from 1979 in which the windows of the coach are blackened over, but at other points it is possible to see "window-pictures," for example, in the hayricks, where there are a number of frames as if they were drawings. The idea is undoubtedly related to the poem he wrote in 1978, *Un disegno nel pagliaio* (A Drawing in the Hayrick), where in a highly metaphorical language Cucchi speaks of the drawing and the hayrick with its paunch covered with thorns.[8]

Cat. 18

Cat. 19

The subject of travel is developed in other drawings in which a locomotive passes through the head of a young boy. In these the observer is irritated not only by

Cat. 29, 30

the disproportionate dimensions, but also by the arbitrary juxtaposition of heterogeneous elements. Each of the drawings seems to have its own meaning, but one we are almost completely unable to decipher. In a song dated 1979, Cucchi wrote: "If you go to where the drawings advance with force along the frontier, you will remember that the world has no end." [9]

Allusions to the meaning are provided also by titles such as *Cavalli di cielo* (Horses of Heaven) or *Le anime viaggiano con i cavalli* (Souls Travel on Horseback), in which a horse with its tail swishing in the wind gallops up a mountainside carrying four small figures, while four heads roll down the slope.[10] A drawing from 1982 shows horses pulling a coach in a headlong career over a field of skulls.[11] The horse is an ambivalent symbol: on the one hand, horses embody the strength of the sun, when they pull the war chariot of the Sun God, and on the other the strength of the moon when they represent the liquid element, the sea, and chaos. Thus the horse is a symbol of both life and death, solar and lunar. In shamanistic beliefs it also acts as the psychopomp or guide of souls to the other world.[12] It is clear from a great number of his works that, either consciously or unconsciously, Cucchi assigns a multiplicity of meanings to the horse. One need only recall *Respiro misterioso* (Mysterious Breath), from 1982, the theme of which is repeated also in a large format drawing, an oil painting, and an etching.[13] With its undulating lines that rise and fall, the "mysterious breath" illustrates respiration which, given the presence of crosses and skulls, seems to allude simultaneously to the rhythms of life and death. In other drawings the horse takes to the air carrying its rider, or ascends vertically from the top of a mountain. In a conversation about his text *Letter from a Drawing at the Front*, in which he speaks of drawings that "make the painter tremble with fear and admiration," Cucchi explained to me that the horse is an animal that awakens in him feelings both of fear and of grandeur, of mystery and energy. "Fear and admiration go together, they liberate each other." [14]

Cat. 86

Cat. 195, 216

In some drawings, the horses "travel" on a boat which provides us with another of Cucchi's important motifs within the theme of travel. Ships, cars, and carts already figured in his early works, such as *Al buio sul mare Adriatico* (In the Dark on the Adriatic Sea), from 1980, a preparatory sketch for the lithograph of the same name contained in the portfolio *Immagine feroce* (Fierce Image),

Cat. 202, 231

Cat. 43

from 1981, in which the "hero" has to sail in a tiny vessel along a narrow sea channel. In the drawing *Portami a terra in un disegno* (Carry me to Earth in a Drawing), from 1978, the sailing boats that appear on the sea are joined, above the masculine figure, to the mountains and the house. In these early drawings Cucchi sets two elementary realities against each other: on the one hand the habitable land with gentle hillsides, trees, houses, and animals; on the other the sea, with boats and waves that advance in a threatening manner. He has spent the better part of his life on the line that divides the land from the sea. Both very soon became two mythical magnitudes in his eyes. Together with woman and the mountains, the sea is "one of the greatest things in life."[15] With this, Cucchi makes repeated and express reference to the Adriatic Sea and the region of The Marches, where he still lives and works most of the year.

Cat. 14

Cat. 47

Since ancient times, journeys by boat or ship have always been an allegory of human life. In the identification between the sea voyage and the destiny of man, both the vessel and the sea are the object of a symbolic interpretation. In *Il sogno del mare* (The Dream of the Sea), from 1983, a sharp, vertical wave rises up from the depths to crash down upon a ship in full sail, which will nevertheless escape from the danger unscathed. In a similar way, in a drawing from 1983 a ship is hurled into the sky, beyond the horizon, by a wave that resembles a gigantic serpent.[16] The vessel heads towards a narrow strait that leads towards the light between mountains of skulls, so that what at first sight appears to be a shipwreck turns out rather to be an "ascension" from this world to the next. In drawing no. 124 of the catalogue another vessel, with its smoking funnel and cross-shaped mast, is literally perched on the top of a mountain, while in a sketch from 1983 the sailor and his boat penetrate an inner space in order to proceed towards a crucifix which, emerging from a whirlpool, becomes a symbol not only of death but also of resurrection. In these drawings Cucchi gives plastic form to dreamlike situations, in that in order to shape his compositions he uses dream structures such as flowing transitions from one place to another, from one time to another, or combinations of plastic elements of different provenances and different levels. Since the description obeys neither lineal nor logical laws, an atmosphere is created which the observer can capture more though association

Cat. 110

Cat. 111

Cat. 120

than through reason, which provides him with new modes of knowledge. In 1984 Cucchi produced *Nel 1984 un millenario trasporto comincia a muoversi attraverso la Preistoria* (In 1984 a Millennial Transport Will Begin Through Prehistory). The frame for this work, made specially for his exhibition in Paris, has the form of a ship, and its subject is a sea voyage of ships and prehistoric animals from island to island. In an interview, Cucchi said the following about the work: "The boat is something metaphysical and although the present object might seem to be so too, the boat is more so...." [17] Later on he said: "The boat is not only related to transport, to the movement of progression, but it even affects the theme of matter in movement...Everything can be transported: thoughts are transported, matter is transported, even we are transported. Everything is a question of movements." [18] In 1986 he presented a whole exhibition devoted to the theme of travel, at the Guggenheim Museum in New York. Regarding its conception he said: "The exhibition is very simple: it's a sign. In this case the sign attracts more than the description or the narration of a story. It symbolizes the path...." [19] Cucchi had provided his canvases with iron wheels, a device he was to repeat in other shows. If at first the drawings were transported by a car or a cart, now they were placed directly on wheels, so that they became vehicles for the journey. Thus the work is the "means of transport" which carries the spiritual message and can lead the artist and the observer to the state of "meraviglia," of admiration and ecstasy. The picture is in itself the vehicle that travels and loads and unloads spiritual elements (see page 10).

As Chinese philosophers had already pointed out, the journey symbolizes the path which is more important than the goal. It is a metaphysical journey, a trip on the sea of life from birth to death; it is the passing of trials and the overcoming of dangers in the search for truth, knowledge and salvation. The journey may imply the "passage" from one plane to another—levels of consciousness, levels of life and the level that goes from life to death—, and may also be the initiation into all these levels. Regarding Ulysses, one of the most famous "travellers," and his Odyssey, Karl Kerényi has written that Homer's work is "not the poem of the heroic life revealed in opposition to inexorable, unavoidable death as its antithesis, but rather the poem of the life impregnated with persistent, omnipresent death. Here the two poles meet. Ulysses' world is the world in suspension on the borderline with death, like the front side of a piece of fabric with its reverse side. This said world is formed both from its backgrounds and undercurrents, those jaws that open behind and below, and from its own reality. Ulysses floats constantly on top of all this.'' [19a]

Tree and Mountain

In the early drawings, the tree is an essential element in Cucchi's repertoire of compositions. In most cases it is a tall, slender cypress; less frequently it is a pine with a parasol-shaped top. The cypress and the pine are trees that Cucchi sees before him daily in the landscape that surrounds him. Furthermore, they are ever-present in the frescoes of the Italian painters of the fourteenth and fifteenth centuries. In his drawings from 1979, it can be seen that these trees already have a special significance for Cucchi. In *Non lo posso dire* (I Cannot Say It), two human heads have been mysteriously encrusted in a cypress that grows tall above a spring. In *Campagna animalosa* (Field of Animals) two trees protectively shelter an inverted head, with which the contrasting movement of the slightly inclined trunks is accentuated. In drawing no. 41, a dense smoke emerges from the cypress and, in combination with that of the house chimney, forms an aureole around the ''stone'' suspended in the air, another leitmotif in the work of Cucchi which will be examined further on. Many of his titles refer to the *santo albero* (Holy Tree), and in a considerable number of works the trees are crowned by halos or are assigned as the attribute of a saint. Through the accentuation of their vertical position it seems that they attempt to make contact with the sky, which would explain why in a considerable number of drawings the trees appear

Cat. 27

Cat. 28

Cat. 41

Cat. 38, 44

Cat. 38, 39

on the top of a mountain. Thus the tree becomes a metaphor in which man can see his existential situation between the earth and heaven.[19b]

Cat. 63, 64

Just as Cucchi's trees are not true trees, neither are his mountains true mountains. Although the rounded hills of his early works are inspired in images of his native land, The Marches, they do not allude to specific hills. In a 1983 interview, Cucchi declared that "a mountain is really boring because it's static and always the same, but it's also incredible because of what it contains, and that creates a state of astonishment in you... I believe that the inner problem is what matters, because what you see has already gone." [20] Thus the artist is not interested in the description of the external appearance of things, since what is seen has by now passed. In his drawings the mountain is a sign in which past and present form a unified whole. For him the mountains belong to the category of "the great things in life," "they are true," they exist and at the same time time they are a "legend." [21] In most of his drawings the mountain has advanced to a position very close to the observer and is projected from the bottom to the top of the frame. Its dark peak, reduced to its essential form and modelled in soft charcoal, stands out crisply against the clear background, without a defined space. Its timeless presence confers upon it a magic radiance. At this time charcoal is Cucchi's favourite medium: "Charcoal is a material that shines within, has eyes. There are colours, such as those of chalk, which are opaque; they have no inner light, they are blind. By contrast, with charcoal I can work even at night." [22] With this medium Cucchi achieves structures reminiscent of Seurat.

Cat. 70, 71

Mountains reveal "saints" on their peaks—*Il miracolo delle montagne* (The Miracle of the Mountains)—or else are joined to them by their feet or their arms.[23] There are those that are even crowned with halos or adorned with crosses, and occasionally from their peaks smoke emerges which, as in volcanoes, attests to the inner, hidden forces of the earth. In *Tutte le montagne sono sante* (All Mountains are Holy), in which the four vertical cypresses establish a direct relationship with the mountains, the title alludes to a spiritual experience. A picture from 1983[24] with a city on top of a mountain is entitled *Più vicino agli dei* (Nearer to the Gods), as if the height represented there made possible an encounter between earth and heaven.

Cat. 72
Cat. 66, 67
Cat. 44, 50, 70
Cat. 40
Cat. 44

Before the mountain peak lies the abyss. In the album *La Scimmia* (The Simian), from 1983, there is a drawing in which a large head is dragged down the mountainside by a whirlwind that carries with it a multitude of skulls into the abyss. In this context the motif of the "falling" is situated, interpreted in a considerable number of works in the figure of Icarus[25] which, the fact is, in Cucchi's works is almost invariably somewhat more complex. Thus, for example, in *Il sogno di un giorno* (The Dream of a Day) the "fire of life" (see page 21) which emerges in the form of smoke from the feet of the armless personage acts only to impulse the downward "journey." The personage plunges into the depths, where however the presence of the "saintly" fish seems to indicate that this fall does not necessarily signify death only, for Jonah too was returned to earth by the whale. The fact that Cucchi's imaginary universe can be interpreted in this way is revealed by certain of his declarations during the course of a conversation, in which he compares his works to caverns: "The pictures are like caverns, gigantic, horrific, overwhelming caverns full of doubts and darkness for all of us. Caverns instill fear, they are full of death, but it is precisely this death that provides the possibility to invent everything anew... It is a descent, an attempt to find a support base in the depths." [26]

Cat. 102

Cat. 91

In the album *La Scimmia*[27], besides views of the abyss there are two paintings in which we see a cockerel take to the air in search of the light, having abandoned a mountain of skulls in one case and a dark circle in the other. Similarly, in the drawing *Accanto allo spirito degli eroi* (Next to the Spirit of Heroes), the cockerel leaves the skulls behind and rises up from the mud like the phoenix from its own ashes. In a poem contained in the album, Cucchi interprets these flights as spiritual manifestations: "I went on my way, then; I came across cocks flying away from the doubt upon the origin. Such flights are important for the twentieth century; they are spiritual demonstrations, different from every worldly taste." In two strongly expressive charcoal drawings from 1984, Cucchi once again tackles the themes of "descent" and "ascent." To do so, in both cases he chose a long, vertical format. In number 132 of the catalogue, belonging to the *Tetto* (Roof) cycle, we see a figure that, in its fall, clings to the mountains with one hand while the other hand stretches outward to fly, as if the personage wanted at the same time to fly from the

Cat. 114

Cat. 132

earth. Thus the ambivalence of both movements is reflected in the representation. At the top we see a dark "passage" peopled with skulls and opening towards the light. One of the figure's eyes, alert and staring, attempts to pierce the darkness of the place. This brings to mind the *tondo* of 1983, *Bisogna togliere i grandi dipinti dal paesaggio* (Great Paintings Must be Removed From the Landscape),[28] in which a large head with its wide-open, horror-struck eye is dragged along by a dark whirlwind. In these two works Cucchi seems to allude to enlightenment through descent.[29] Similarly ambivalent is the figure that floats and ascends in the drawing from the *Italia* series. With arms upraised and impelled by the smoke from the small vessel that sails below, this figure attempts to reach the upper regions, although the side of its body is still part of the mountains: a saint with stigmata on his hands and feet who tries to overcome terrestrial limits in order to achieve spiritual liberty and enlightenment. Through the projection of heterogeneous elements of different sizes, joined to concentration into a few "signs," Cucchi manages in a convincing way to visualize certain spiritual contents. Generally speaking the descent to the depths, to the chasm, seems to be connected to ideas of reincarnation and immortality; on the other hand, however, it could also mean the search for one's own self.[30] Immersion in water can be interpreted as the "return to the primitive being of all forms and the recovery of an undifferentiated existence prior to life on this earth... The act of appearing on the surface reproduces the cosmogonical process of the emergence of forms; immersion is a kind of dissolving of these forms. For this reason water, as a symbol, contains both death and rebirth of life. Contact with water always produces a regeneration: on the one hand because dissolving is followed by a 'new birth,' and on the other because immersion brings the force of life to fruition and causes it to multiply."[31] It is especially necessary for the artist to submerge himself time and time again in the depths if he is to renew his creative forces.

Cat. 131

House

The house in its most elementary form, generally long and narrow, is a constant element in the image universe of Cucchi's earliest works (see frontispiece). However, his house is not only a place that offers protection and refuge, but also a corner inhabited by imagination and mystery: *Le case si riempiono* (The Houses are Filling Themselves) is the title of a drawing from 1980[32], while a song from 1979 begins with the words *Le case si riempiono tutte a mezza altezza* (The Houses are Filling Themselves at Mid Height).[33] "I don't believe there can be an empty house...," says Cucchi. "A house has a sense of form, it is a place where one can breathe, breathe in a filled place." [34] In another passage, he says: "I can fill only a half...In the other half it is possible to travel: there is air, time, space." [35] In the drawing *La scopa dell'amore* (The Sweeping Brush of Love), from 1979, a long staircase leads to the very highly placed entrance to a house which, nevertheless, seems to be accessible only once one has managed to get past a strange animal perched on a rock in front.[36] The distant objective of all desires—the image of a woman with a house and a mountain—appears as a medallion in the form of a window. Occasionally the house slips onto the water like a boat, thus becoming an element in the theme of the journey. Its meaning depends always on the context. Like a spotlight, it can be projected from the summit of a mountain until it gives the impression of wanting to reach the heaven: "Houses are Filling Themselves in Heaven." The house extends between different spaces and different times. When as a form it is projected upwards, it becomes a metaphor that illustrates man's search for transcendence. In drawing number 103 in the catalogue, three houses contained within a triangle form a precinct for a group of vociferating heads, and the only possible way out from here is a narrow opening. Could this be the "dismal place" from the poem *La Scimmia*, where the artist finds the "thoughts of painters"? "The entrance had become so narrow that it was scarcely possible to enter." [37]
In other drawings that belong to the *La Scimmia* series, the houses collapse and bury a head, or else they are so close together that the head is almost squashed: with a mournful expression it slowly slides toward a river of skulls. In these works the head has a special significance. Its destiny is the destiny the whole human

Cat. 7, 32
Cat. 33
Cat. 233
Cat. 81
Cat. 101
Cat. 104
Cat. 100

being. It is as if journeys were made in the head. They are spiritual journeys or journeys in dreams, as can be appreciated in the large format drawing in the Kunsthaus in Zurich: here the sleeping head sees in a dream the vision of a small boat.[38] Its title, *Disegno tonto* (Stupid Drawing), is by no means fortuitous. Here the adjective "stupid" must be understood as an allusion to prerational, prelogical structures, rather than as the opposite of "intelligent." Through modifications to its external form, its placing, and its facial expression, the head can transmit a constant stream of new contents. Haggard, decomposed, careworn, it often presents traits that bring to mind a self-portrait. In reference to the etching *Un'immagine oscura* (A Dark Image), in which a large head with a sorrowful expression is seen at the top of an elongated house, Cucchi writes: "A face exuding joyful pain and painful joy."[44] The "journey" from one plane to another is always accompanied by pain and joy, by *paura e meraviglia*, as Cucchi said on a certain occasion: "Fear and miracle go together: they liberate each other."[14] Mircea Eliade describes the "ascension" experience in a similar way: "...and the approach to this reality awakens in the profane conscience an ambivalent feeling of fear and joy, of attraction and rejection...."[39]

Comparable experiences seem to serve as the basis for drawing number 90 of the catalogue. Here the houses are launched into the heights by swirling clouds of smoke, while a lightning stroke falls and lights up the red figure in the foreground, causing it to fall backwards with such violence that the only things visible are the legs, suspended in the air, and a foot that emits a supernatural beam of light. Furthermore, while in the houses we have seen hitherto the windows were almost always dark, in this drawing there is an abundance of strikingly "illuminated" ones. This illustration of a spiritual experience is reminiscent of Caravaggio, a painter of whom Cucchi often speaks. Caravaggio's *The Conversion of St. Paul* (Church of Santa Maria del Popolo, Rome) transmits with such force the idea of the spiritual enlightenment of Saul, thrown backwards by his horse, that we need not be surprised to find echoes of this in Cucchi's vision.[40]

Cat. 90

As in this painting, in many drawings clouds of smoke are a characteristic element. Smoke emerges from houses, and the locomotive gives off smoke, as do the boat and the chimney . All this is perfectly natural and causes no surprise;

Cat. 7, 32

Cat. 29, 30

however, trees also give off smoke and smoke emerges from the feet of the falling figure, that falls from the mountains or from the skulls, dragging houses along with it to the heights. It is possible to appreciate in these images the presence of occult forces and spiritual energies. Like the trees and the houses, the smoke rises up into the air, as if attempting to establish contact with infinity. By nature it is linked to fire and therefore forms part of its multiple symbolism. For Cucchi smoke proceeds from the "fire of life" (*il fuoco della vita*) and signifies vitality, while fire is a "natural, vital, and dynamic element." [41] For this reason he sees in them not a destructive element but rather the force of renovation of life. In number 131 in the catalogue, smoke impels the ascent of the "resuscitated one" (see page 18) who it seems first had to descend to Hades and submit to the rites of purification and transformation.

Cat. 41

Cat. 91

Oval Object

Great oval objects that resist unequivocal interpretations have become a constant leitmotif in the work of Cucchi. In some drawings, for example, by virtue of their consistency we see them as stones, in others as living matter that bring feminine symbols to mind, while in yet others they hang in the air like clouds. Their appearance and meaning vary according to the composition, but they always have an air of mystery about them, and are often somewhat unexpected and threatening.

Cat. 41, 44

In the drawing *Santo Albero* (Sacred Tree), from 1980, the "saint" turns toward the ball-shaped object in an attitude of fervor, but he dares not touch it; to a certain extent this occurs also in the large format drawing from the same year, *C'è del santo tra le mani* (Something Sacred Between the Hands),[42] in which

Cat. 38

the man's hands approach the object as if under a spell, trying to discover the secret contained inside. This "something sacred between the hands" can become a halo or "sacred bread," which reveals its force as nourishment for the soul. Stones are often images of the *ego* and perhaps symbolize "the most elementary and at the same time most profound intuition of the eternal and of the immutable that man can ever have." [42a] From among the variety of symbols represented by the stone, that of the philosopher's stone is a well-known image of inner integrity. The feminine symbolism of the oval object is confirmed in several works, in which male symbols also appear and allusions are often made to a battle between the sexes. In drawing number 65 of the catalogue, the hunter aims his gun directly at the egg perched on his foot.[43] In drawing number 60 the egg and the small tree in the form of a phallus are joined by a line of "attraction," while the animal in the pine sends its "breath," adorned with three halos, toward the egg. For Cucchi the woman represents cycles. Like animals, "the woman is a reference to the universe, has creation inside her." [41] By contrast, men are anonymous: "Men are painters, cyclists, climbers, game wardens, sailors, hunters, warriors." Only through creative work is it possible for the artist to establish contact with the cycle of life.

Cat. 54, 55
Cat. 74
Cat. 65
Cat. 60

In many drawings a mysterious energy allows the "stone" to float, the materialization of all eager searches for transcendence. In the poem *Un'immagine oscura*, from 1982, which refers to the large format etching of the same title in which a large black stone floats over the landscape, Cucchi writes: "An infinitely wide sea of black stones which are devoured mysteriously to become a black mass in the sky." [44] These words remind us that the stone also forms part of the cycle of death and resurrection, a fact confirmed in the Guggenheim Museum exhibition in 1986. Here the stone appeared in the form of a bronze sculpture placed on the floor and consisting of two pieces, each of which "incubates" an embryonic figure[45] in a reference to birth and revival.

Cat. 80, 137, 138

Similar ideas are expressed in the drawings produced for the "Sculpture for Basle" in 1984. The "stone-clouds" that float over a desolate, barren landscape then descend to earth and settle on hillsides of skulls. Their dense, organic forms, on the other hand, suggest that they grow on the "calvaries," thus

Cat. 148, 149

linking them to the idea of the appearance of a new life after death. This interpretation is supported by a drawing[46] that brings to mind the work of Munch. Here we see small shoots that sprout up on a mushroom-shaped mountainside covered with skulls. Something similar occurs in drawing number 150, while in number 151 there are also organic forms that project upwards. By contrast, in number 153 the head is impaled on four houses in the form of stakes. This ambivalence between the organic and the inorganic is later transposed to the sculpture, at whose mast a staircase with skulls appears and winds up to the top like a serpent. In the book *Ewige Bilder und Sinnbilder*, Mircea Eliade alludes to the meaning of the staircase as the symbol of ascent in all archaic cultures: "It is the plastic illustration of the rupture of the plane that makes the transformation possible from one way of being to another; or, if we take the situation of the cosmological plane as our starting point, it makes movement possible between Heaven, the Earth and Hell." [47] In this context it is extremely significant that the two masts of Basle emerge from a "hollow" in the form of a crater. "A look into its interior is a look into the interior of the Earth... In its diffuse depths the residues of geology are amalgamated." [48] "Descent into the nether world" would seem to be a prerequisite in order subsequently to accede to the staircase of Heaven. The symbolism of the staircase is made manifest in an early work, *La scopa dell'amore* (see p. 19), and in drawing number 263 in the catalogue, in which the embryonic figure looks into the mirror at the head of the staircase.

Cat. 33

Giulio Cesare Roma

Between 1983 and 1984 Enzo Cucchi created the *Giulio Cesare Roma* (Julius Caesar Rome) cycle.[49] During this period the artist spent long periods in Rome and lived at first hand the grandiose history of the city.[50] In order to show me the proximity between past and present, during my visit Cucchi took me to see the palaces of the Renaissance, whose formerly sumptuous inner courtyards are now occupied by families swarming with children, and showed me how in many places remains of antiquity still show beside present-day constructions. "Everywhere there are skulls beneath the ground," he says. Cucchi is fascinated by the strata of vanished cultures upon which new life has been built. This he expresses very directly in his prospectuses of the city, retouched with collage, in which for example he places a "stratum" of his own, covered with skulls, on top of the old Coliseum.[51] The skulls should be understood not only as symbols of death, but also as part of the cycle of life according to Cucchi's conception: "I'm convinced that art is really full of death, but it is a death that also constitutes an idea of reinvention...I contemplate death according to a vitality, a new creation." [52] For this reason the skull is not for him a symbol of the *vanitas* that makes all human activity ephemeral, but rather a metaphor of vital energy that feeds on itself and survives the destruction of our time.[53] This is revealed in drawing number 96 in the catalogue, which shows us the dark subterranean vaults of the catacombs. In this "nether world" we see a cart loaded with heads being pulled by a flaming horse, the guide of souls, while the cloud of smoke points towards the heights in its upward movement.

Cat. 95

Cucchi's European consciousness is also accentuated during this period. In the poem *Hotel* for the *Giulio Cesare Roma* catalogue, we read the following: "In the hills, along river banks and shores, in the cradle of the Mediterranean, for centuries painters have developed that sense of art that enlightens the world with paintings...Painters of ancient Europe are grouped in this sphere, and move and transform it into frescoes, paintings and clay figures." For this reason, let no one think it purely fortuitous that during this same period representations of the geographical outline of Italy appear in Cucchi's work.

Vitebsk/Harar

As from 1983 Cucchi has shown an increasing tendency to group his paintings and drawings in series — he calls them families — and to present his exhibitions under a single leitmotif. Thus in 1984 he put together an exhibition entitled *Vitebsk/Harar* in the Sperone/Westwater Gallery in New York, and in 1985 he showed his works in the Galerie Templon, Paris, under the title of *Arthur Rimbaud au Harar*. Harar is the African locality to which Rimbaud retired having written *Une saison en enfer* and *Illuminations*, two model exponents of "descent" and "ascent." It seems that the poet subsequently gave up writing. Figures such as Rimbaud "cannot be valued according totally to aesthetic patterns, since they seek a deep relationship between life and work," says Cucchi. "They search for communication with the global form of things....He wanted to accede to the profound fixed points of his existence."[54] To this southern location, Harar, Cucchi places a northern counterpoint, Vitebsk, the Russian city of Malevich and the suprematist Utopia. But in the same way that the landscape of The Marches does not form a real setting in Cucchi's work, so Africa and Russia are for him imaginary places. In his drawings they appear as barren, desert regions dominated by solitude and death. Small deserted houses either rise up beside enormous conglomerations of stones or else, arranged on top of each other in horizontal blocks, they move like a spaceship toward a light-colored crater. This is a new, astonishing invention of his. Equally new is the representation of skulls that ascend vertically, dragging a tail behind them, as symbol of the vital energy that feeds on itself. The "ascent," which in a way is illustrated in movement, acquires as a result an extraordinary dynamic force. This can be appreciated especially in drawing no. 144 in the catalogue, in which an enormous skull with a long trail rises up, together with smaller skulls, against dramatic escarpments which seem still to be in their formation stage. Their toothed crests introduce a type of mountain hitherto unseen in Cucchi's work. The series *Vitebsk/Harar* reflects also the role of the artist today: he is seated at the piano, completely alone in a desolate landscape peopled only by skulls, but in which the dark, flaming curtain is drawn back, allowing him to see an enlightening view. Cucchi speaks constantly of the end of painting, but

Cat. 117, 118

Cat. 139-147 and 204-206

Cat. 146

Cat. 143, 144

he places his hopes on the renovation of the "picture," of the "sign": "In order to check storms, catastrophes, earthquakes, it is said every day throughout the world that one day painters... sailors, will create allegories capable to setting the course; this is a difficult task, a complicated process of sensitivity." [55]

34 Drawings Sing

Barren landscapes and angry seas also characterize the settings of the series *34 disegni cantano* (34 Drawings Sing), from 1985. The craggy mountain formations reminiscent of icebergs bring to mind (and this is no coincidence) Leonardo da Vinci's drawings of The Flood. On a desolate ground, windowless houses bend beneath the action of an invisible force, and enormous, vertical heads, hard and clear in outline and almost invariably without facial features, emerge directly from the ground. This nightmarish atmosphere reaches singular heights in a drawing in which we see a quasi-human figure caught in a raging whirlwind that razes everything to the ground and makes the whole earth tremble; we know that the terrified figure will soon be dragged down to the depths. Furthermore, in the sky the whirlwind itself takes the form of a horrific face, seen as if in a vision. In 1978 Cucchi had already given visual form to a similar experience. The whirlwind in *Vento di vino*[56] (Wind of Wine or Divine Wind), which fills the whole sheet with swirling turbulence and tears trees from the ground, inexorably drags a man, who struggles in vain, down into the abyss. In this drawing too a face appears above—childlike this time—and there is also a floating "saintly figure." Squalls of wind, as a "circular, solar and creative movement," symbolize ascent and descent.[57] C.G. Jung describes the dream of a man who finds himself on a slope and decides to go down to the dark lake in the valley. "When he reaches the edge, everything becomes dark and dismal,

Cat. 170

Cat. 13

and suddenly a violent gust of air sweeps the surface of the waters. Panic overcomes him." Jung continues: "The dreamer penetrates his own depths and the path leads him to mysterious waters... However, the unearthly wind that rushes over the dark waters is something frightening, like everything whose cause is beyond our ken or our understanding. All this suggests an invisible presence, an inspiration." [58]

In the *34 disegni cantano* series these nightmarish scenes alternate with signs of ascent, such as houses that search for the heights, or rocky mountains that rise up like cathedrals towards the vertiginous heights of the "stone-clouds." In other drawings the landscape appears to be purified. Two vast rocks are reflected in the mirror-like surface of calm waters, and a figure bends over to touch the ground in the center of a "cosmic landscape." It could be said that at this point earth and sky have come together in a rainbow. The posture of the figure brings to mind the text of the manifesto prepared by Corà and Cucchi: "We salute the islands where adventurous landings make it possible for those who are avid for discovery to find themselves, but only if they bow in gratitude and touch the ground with their lips." [59] Regarding this point, the artist expresses himself even more explicitly in one of his drawings from the *Solchi d'Europa* cycle.

Cat. 164
Cat. 175
Cat. 184
Cat. 215

A new motif appears in some drawings, in the form of small trembling figures who gather at the "place of the miracle." Among the creatures they encounter in their path are the mysterious dogs which, like Cerberus, seem to guard the gates to Hell. Every time that Cucchi no longer defines his figures by means of a single line and depicts them by means of short, parallel strokes with which the outline becomes blurred, he manages to express his protagonists' state of agitation. If we attempt to identify ourselves with the diminutive and nervous figure, and consequently capture the full grandeur of the surrounding rocks, we realize that these spaces are unreal: they do not belong to this world. They illustrate "moments between the past and the present that generate the future" (see page 7). The artist moves in great chronological spaces. Mario Diacono once said that Cucchi expresses our fears of the future in paintings of the past. "Disaster as such does not interest me; I am concerned with how the Earth's energy emerges at the surface, how it becomes visible." [60] On examining his

Cat. 179
Cat. 225

34 disegni cantano cycle, we discover indeed that in contrast to landscapes that appear ravished by catastrophes, there are always signs of an opposite movement, so that here too there are illustrations of the cycle of disappearance and renovation, of death and new life. "Yes," says Cucchi, "it's like the story of Orpheus."

In 1985 a bent figure with its spinal column clearly marked began to appear in different contexts. Today we can say that this figure represents the artist himself. In drawing number 199 of the catalogue he is seated on the ridge of a roof, reaching out avidly to grab the black birds as if he wanted them to carry him to Heaven. In another drawing he is stretched out on a grille like St. Laurence, while his naked back irradiates a halo-like light. The figure of *Harar, A.R.* is bent so far forward that it forms a semicircle. "From the formal point of view it resembles the universe. And it could not be any other way. It's a sign" (Enzo Cucchi). This brings to mind *Parapetto occidentale* (Western Parapet), in which Cucchi writes: "Today I imagine the body of a painter curved like the sky above a table; the table legs support the earth."[61] This description of the nature of the painter alludes even more clearly to the drawing *Siamo nell'abisso del vedere?* (Are We in the Abyss of Sight?), produced in the summer of 1987 for the journal "Flash Art," and whose title refers to enlightenment in descent (see page 18 and following). Here the figure with its radiant spinal column is in the centre of a hollow which progressively opens towards clarity, from which beams of white points emerge, terminating in the figure. This alludes to a new "sign" which Cucchi has been using as a leitmotif since 1986. He calls it the *cosmic line*, and it consists of a line of dots reminiscent of rosary beads and which goes beyond the limits of the figures themselves. In connection with this, the spinal column of the figures appears as the *cosmic line* of the human being, a metaphor of the duality of man between Earth and Heaven. However, in this figure Cucchi searches for something else. He wants his inclination to be understood as a sacrifice, as a renunciation and as an idea of consummation.[62] Here begins a tendency which will define Cucchi's work with progressively greater strength. In his latest major text, published in 1987 and entitled *Sparire* (To Disappear), he writes the following: "This is why one remains in this territory closed off to relations outside; in order once again to find form in the interior of things, to

Cat. 234

Cat. 198

Cat. 224, 229

submerge oneself...to float...to disappear. In order to find a plane, a sign that marks." The movements of floating and disappearing appear as themes in numerous drawings from 1986. Diminutive creatures formed exclusively from a dot representing the head and a stroke acting as the body float between the sky and the earth and disappear into the infinite heights. They are related to the rudimentary creatures in the plastic works for Venice and Louisiana which Cucchi calls *Esserini*. Nevertheless, even more closely related to these ideas is the space that Cucchi created in 1988 especially for our exhibition and which he calls *La disegna*, a name he would like to apply to the show as a whole. *La disegna*, a name Cucchi has created, for him signifies "the mother of all drawings." The space contains three large works in white rubber, above which the paintings appear as drawings in relief. Cucchi says that rubber is ideal not only for this kind of commitment and this concept of drawing but also as a mental form. However, it lacks value as a material. What is important is what is drawn. "It's only a drawing, a drawing that moves, that floats. The same image appears on different planes." To be honest, the male figure in the first painting is the largest and the one nearest to the observer. It occupies the whole height of the canvas, and its oblique position suggests that it is emerging from the frame. In the following painting two smaller figures can be seen, clearly based on the same model, while the third features the smallest figure of all, attempting to escape upward from the top part of the work. What most attracts the attention, however, is the fact that in all the works the right-hand side is completely empty. "The drawing moves, floats, disappears, appears and literally disappears in the work itself. It's a conceptual game, a kind of moving forward today...." In this space, with the visual expression of different states Cucchi has created an impressive sign of the cycle of life and death; in other words, of the renewal of life as the aftermath of death.[63]

Cat. 227, 231, 237

At a time when the world is becoming increasingly threatened by ecological, economic, and military conflicts, when poverty and ensuing death form part of the day-to-day experience of wide sectors of the population, and when the fears and alienation of humanity grow as people find themselves more and more at the mercy of anonymous power structures in modern society,[64] Cucchi draws signs of hope in works of an apparently apocalyptical nature. "It is not a question of describing chaos, senseless ambition or hope; the beauty of painting has also deceived us and brought us disappointments. Surprisingly enough, needs point towards a new space between the kingdom of chaos and the decorative order. The space of deliberately sought ambiguity.''[65] For Cucchi this space means not participation without commitment to life, without a point of view, but the struggle to overcome the dangers of a world organized in a purely rational and technocratic way, and the will to recover spiritual forces which will perhaps help us to find new paths. His works attest to the vigor with which he searches for these paths. The artist's task is rooted in his life and in the culture to which he belongs as a result of his own personal history and that of his forebears. In Cucchi's work both branches come together to form a symbolic universe in which both individual and collective inner images take shape. And this explains the plurality of each symbol. For this reason, within the framework of this present analysis the only viable alternative has been to select certain symbols representative of his activities and present them in accordance with an interpretative focus that respects the essentially open character of the work of art. The commentaries offered here are not exhaustive, nor do they possess the depth they would have had if religious or psychoanalytic aspects of the personality of the artist had been contemplated. This, however, is not the art historian's task. The important thing is to observe how the artist acts as the container, or, in Cucchi's words, as the means of transport thanks to which the language of symbols becomes translated into new forms of knowledge.

NOTES

1. In 1974 Pier Paulo Pasolini wrote the following in an article about Ignazio Buttitta, a famous Italian poet who writes in dialect: "One of the many tragedies we have been forced to live through in recent years (and which I have lived through in a totally personal and physical way) is the tragic loss of dialect as one of the most sorrowful moments of loss of reality (which in Italy has always been determined in a particularist, decentralized and concrete way, never centralized or determined 'from above')." Reproduced in *Freibeuterschiften*, Berlin, 1978, p. 106.

2. Enzo Cucchi, *Guida al disegno* (Munich: Kunsthalle Bielefeld/Staatsgalerie moderner Kunst, 1987), p. 12 ff.

3. Enzo Cucchi, *Solchi d'Europa*, 17/9/1985, Munich: AEIUO, 1985, pp. 24-17.

4. *Ein Gespräch - una discussione: Joseph Beuys, Jannis Kounellis, Anselm Kiefer, Enzo Cucchi*, Zurich, 1986, p. 50.

5. *Quartetto: Joseph Beuys, Enzo Cucchi, Luciano Fabro, Bruce Nauman*, Venice, 1984, no. 30, no. 27, and no. 21.

6. From: *Sparire = Entschwinden = To Disappear*, Ancona: 1987; New York: 1987.

7. *Solchi d'Europa*, pp. 14-16.

8. *Tre o quattro artisti secchi*, (Modena: Emilio Mazzoli Editore, 1978). Reproduced in Enzo Cucchi, *La cerimonia delle cose*, (New York, 1985), p. 28: "The thorny belly around the hayrick was beside itself. But it managed to get a drawing out of us."

9. Seven young artists from Italy, Kunsthalle Basel; Museum Folkwang, Essen; Stedelijk Museum, Amsterdam, 1980, p. 27.

10. Enzo Cucchi, *Zeichnungen* (Kunsthaus Zürich/Groninger Museum, 1982), p. 59.

11. Enzo Cucchi, *Un'immagine oscura*, (Essen: Museum Folkwang, 1982), p. 23.

12. J.C. Cooper, *Illustriertes Lexikon der traditionellen Symbole* (Wiesbaden, 1986), p. 138.

13. Zurich, 1982, catalogue no. 37, plate on p. 75, "Respiro misterioso," 1983, oil. Reproduced in *Flash Art*, summer 1987, p. 75. See also *Il respiro del cavallo*, 1982, etching, and *Untitled*, 1980, aquatint, plates 15 and 6 in *Etchings and Lithographs*, 1979-1985, Munich, 1985.

14. Author's conversation with Enzo Cucchi in Ancona, 1982.

15. Catalogue Kunsthaus Zurich, *op. cit.* 1982, p. 9.

16. Compare the stimulus through a drawing by Victor Hugo: "Est ou animal fabuleux," 1866-1868, in *Victor Hugo, Phantasien in Tusche* (Kunsthaus Zürich, 1987), catalogue no. 51, plate on p. 31.

17. Quoted in *Enzo Cucchi: Testa* (Munich: Städtische Galerie im Lenbachhaus, 1987), p. 109.

18. *Ibid.* p. 110.

19. "La Stampa," 3/5/1986, quoted in *Testa*, p. 127.

19a. Wolfgang Bauer, Irmtraud Dümotz, and Sergius Colowin, *Lexikon der Symbole* (Wiesbaden, 1984), p. 176 ff.

19b. There is an interesting allusion here to Humbert de Superville, for which I have my colleague Bernhard von Waldkirch to thank. In his *Essai sur les signes inconditionnels dans l'art* (Leiden: C.C. van der Hoek, 1827-1832), Superville elaborates a system of signs based on sensitivity or, more specifically, on consciousness: "Man is erect and turned towards the sky. He is erect because the longitudinal axis of his body, the prolongation of a radius of our globe, is perpendicular to the plane of the horizon. He is turned towards the sky because the direction of this axis situates the zenith above his head: two characters contained implicitly one in the other and rigorously different. Thus man seems to rise to the vault of Heaven as if from the center of the Earth, and cover the whole space contained within its two extremes. His physical strength and dignity, the result of his walking erect, become the guarantees of his moral strength and dignity, and thus the whole of Man becomes contained in the expression of his own Axis, the unique, sole primitive and absolute vertical direction." (Quoted in *Mondrian: From Figuration to Abstraction*, The Hague: Gemeentemuseum, 1988, p. 172 ff).

20. Interview with Giancarlo Politi and Helena Kontova in *Flash Art*, No. 114 (Nov. 1983), p. 16.

21. Author's interview with Enzo Cucchi in Ancona, 1982.

22. Catalogue Kunsthaus Zurich, *op. cit.* 1982, p. 12.

23. Cucchi makes use here of an idea by René Magritte—*The Red Shoes*—although he does not allow the feet, now green, to become boots. The dreamlike, irrational atmosphere is achieved by means of the sudden cutting of the legs and the juxtaposition in the painting of heterogeneous elements.

24. *Enzo Cucchi* (New York: Solomon R. Guggenheim Museum, 1986), catalogue 35.

25. Catalogue Kunsthaus Zurich, 1982, p. 8 and plate on p. 15: *I soli vuoti* (The Empty Suns), 1980; also Helmut Friedel in *Der Traum des Orpheus* (Munich: Städtische Galerie im Lenbachhaus, 1984), p. 164. It is highly significant that Cucchi should have adopted a figure from Giotto's *The Last Judgment* for the personage that falls in *Pesce in schiena del mare adriatico* (Helmut Friedel, p. 164), although he interprets it in his own way, since instead of a snake there is a fish around the neck. (Capella degli Scrovegni, Padua, plate XXXIX in *Klassiker der Kunst, Das Gesemtwerk von Giotto*, Milan, 1966.)

26. *Testa*, 1987, Vol. 1, p. 113.

27. Enzo Cucchi, *La Scimmia* (The Simian) portfolio (New York: Sperone/ Westwater, 1983).

28. *Parkett*, No. 1 (1984), p. 65.

29. See *Siamo nell'abisso del vedere?* (Are We in the Abyss of Seeing?), p. 32. Regarding the existential experience of being dragged down into the abyss, there is an interesting analogy in E.A. Poe's story "A Descent Into the Maelstrom," in which a fisherman who has been trapped in a whirlpool manages to save his own life thanks to his acute observations. (See Jeannot Simmen, "Vertigo und moderne Plastik," in *Beiträge zu Kunst und Kunstgeschichte um 1900*, Schweizerisches Institut für Kunstwissenschaft, 1984-1986 annual, Zurich: 1986, p. 128.)

30. *Lexikon der Symbole*, *op. cit.*, p. 149.

31. Mircea Eliade, *Ewige Bilder und Sinnbilder: Über die magischreligiöse Symbolik* (Frankfurt am Main, 1986), p. 167.

32. Catalogue Kunsthaus Zurich, 1982, p. 31.

33. Enzo Cucchi, *La cerimonia delle cose*, 1985, p. 34.

34. Interview with Cucchi in *Enzo Cucchi* (Madrid: Fundación Caja de Pensiones, Madrid, 1986), p. 109.

35. Journal Wolkenkratzer 12, 1986, p. 77.

36. See the interpretation of Mario Diacono as a sphinx (*cagna alata* = winged bitch) in the installation *La Cavalla azzurra, 1978-1979*, in *Verso una nuova Iconografia* (Collezione Tauma, 1984), p. 148.

37. *La Scimmia*: "A dismal place, a sewer; I have found it together with the thoughts of painters."

38. Catalogue Kunsthaus Zurich, 1982, p. 60.

39. Mircea Eliade, *op. cit.*, p. 56.

40. *L'opera completa del Caravaggio, Classici dell'Arte*, (Milan: Rizzoli, 1967), plate XXXVII (1600-1601).

41. Conversation between the author and Cucchi, Ancona, 1982.

42. Catalogue Kunsthaus Zurich, 1982, p. 7.

42a. C.G. Jung, *Bewusstes und Unbewusstes* (Frankfurt am Main, 1957), p. 210.

43. See analogous treatments in the large format *Olé* drawings, 1980, Zurich, 1982, p. 34, and catalogue 20, p. 69.

44. Catalogue Museum Folkwang, Essen, 1982, p. 29, plate p. 31.

45. New York, 1986, pp. 196/197; see also Martin Schwander, *Enzo Cucchi: scultura 1982-1988* (Munich, 1988), p. 57, as well as no. 217 in this book.

46. Catalogue Museum Folkwang, Essen, 1982, p. 21.

47. Mircea Eliade, *op. cit.*, p. 55.

48. Martin Schwander, *op. cit.*, p. 34.

49. The exhibition of the same title took place in 1983-1984 in the Stedelijk Museum, Amsterdam, and in 1984 at the Kunsthalle in Basle.

50. In a conversation with Demosthenes Davvetas, he said, "Memory is an indispensable part of pictorial creation." Similarly, "For me history is a memory. Remembrances are memory. When you speak of Napoleon, for example, and I talk to you about Julius Caesar, neither of us knew the one or the other. All we know are echoes, something strange. This means that we should therefore not take history in its literal sense." In *Malerei—Peinture—Painting*, No. 2 (1986), p. 6.

51. The "Testa" exhibition, Munich, 1987, revealed a similar procedure in the elaboration of an old theater prospect in Rome. "Through the impression of enormous feet Cucchi creates a new imaginist plane in that he breaks the illusionism of the painting. The eternal city becomes ground, a 'human' basis for existence, created by the deposits of history, on which only now solid settlement and progress are possible." Helmut Friedel, *op. cit.*, vol. II, p. 14.

52. From a conversation with Jörg Zutter in January 1985, quoted in the brochure *Enzo Cucchi* (Basle: Museum für Gegenwartskunst, 1986).

53. Mario Diacono, *Vitebsk/Harar*, New York, 1984, quoted in: Madrid, 1986, p. 61. Here Cucchi also says "The cemetery is part of my landscape: it is one of the things I know best; I have always lived in villages where the cemetery was the most important thing there was. Skulls are often found in the country side. It is a primary image, not a subject... My cemetery is alive. Everything in it is related."

54. Enzo Cucchi in *Malerei*, No. 2 (1986), p. 2.

55. Enzo Cucchi, *Giulio Cesare Roma* (Basle: Kunsthalle, 1984).

56. The title is phonetically ambiguous. It can be translated as "Wind of Wine" or as "Wind Divine."

57. Cooper, *op. cit.*, p. 215.

58. C.G. Jung, *op. cit.*, p. 26.

59. *Solchi d'Europa*, p. 35.

60. Catalogue Madrid, 1986, p. 113.

61. Catalogue Solomon R. Guggenheim Museum, New York, 1986, p. 210: "Io oggi immagino il corpo di un pittore incurvato sopra un tavolo come un cielo: le zampe del tavolo sostengono la terra."

62. Conversation with the author in Rome, 1988.

63. The heart-shaped "stones" that the male figures hold in their hands contain images, in the same way that in their bellies images are reflected: they carry this image inside them. Cucchi has always insisted that "a picture is born in the belly, not in the head." (*Ritratto di casa*, 1978: *La cerimonia delle cose, op. cit.*, p. 24).

64. See Horst Petri, *Angst und Frieden: Psychoanalyse und gesellschaftliche Verantwortung* (Frankfurt am Main, 1987).

65. Enzo Cucchi in *Sparire, op. cit.*

L'idea di un disegno è l'unica possibilità, per un uomo, di pensare. Un uomo eretto, in equilibrio, è l'unica possibilità di pensare a una forma o di avere un'immagine; l'unica idea per pensare alla distanza tra una cosa e l'altra. È l'idea di un disegno. Visto che la realtà esterna ha vinto, solo un uomo sconfitto vi può andare incontro come al ritorno orgoglioso dalla sconfitta, decidendo di mettere gli uomini di pensiero di fronte a un albero a parlare con lui. Solo così possono ristabilire i tempi e le distanze e i pesi tra se stessi e il loro pensiero e ritrovare un territorio in cui pensare di nuovo un'immagine necessaria, un territorio da giungla, chiuso all'esterno vincente e più fantasioso ormai di qualsiasi artista. L'unica antenna, l'unica compagnia e armonia resta un albero, come la coda del cane. Solo nel rifiuto del dialogo e con l'aiuto di immagini, gli uomini di pensiero si ritroveranno. C'è un posto migliore che davanti a un albero, a parlare con lui?
Come i fiorentini decidevano di prendere il David di Michelangelo e portarlo nella loro piazza, così si dovrebbe decidere di prendere gli uomini di pensiero e isolarli dall'esterno infinitamente più forte di loro e portarli davanti a un albero. La sua ombra è la salvezza dell'arte e del pensiero, che hanno sempre cercato la luce. Ma gli uomini da sempre portano tutto all'ombra.

Enzo Cucchi

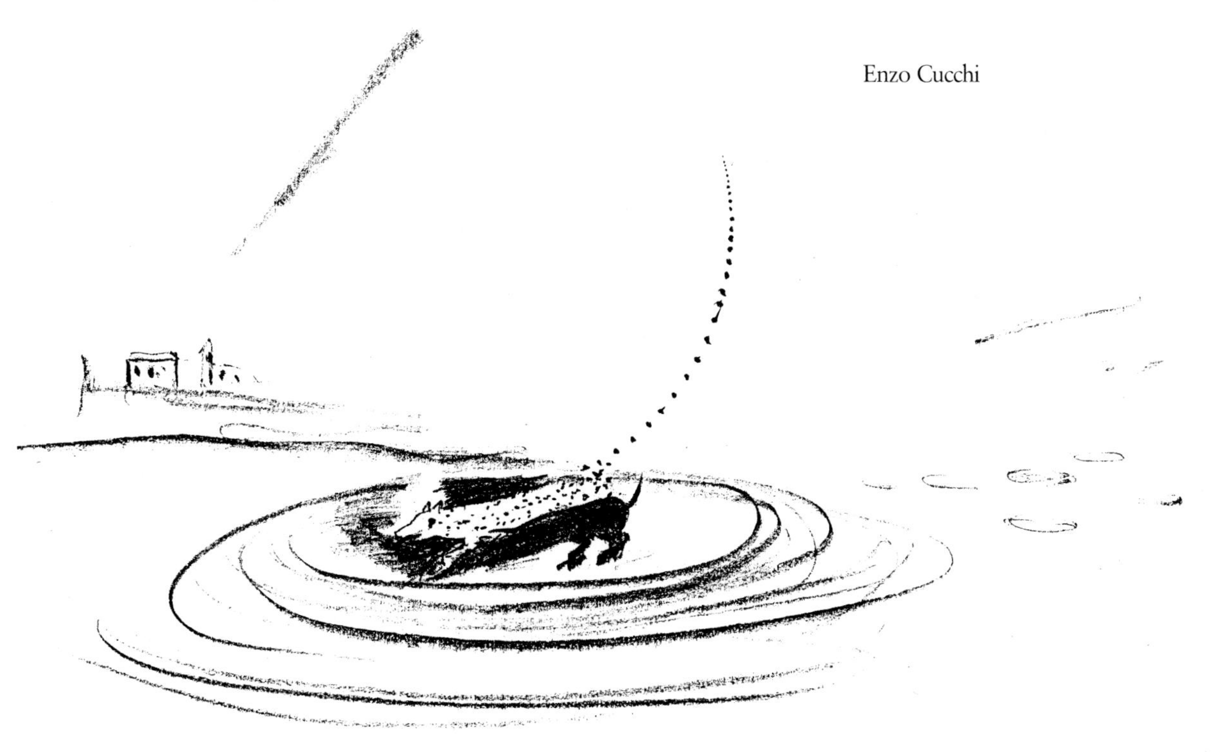

1975

1. *Untitled*. 1975.

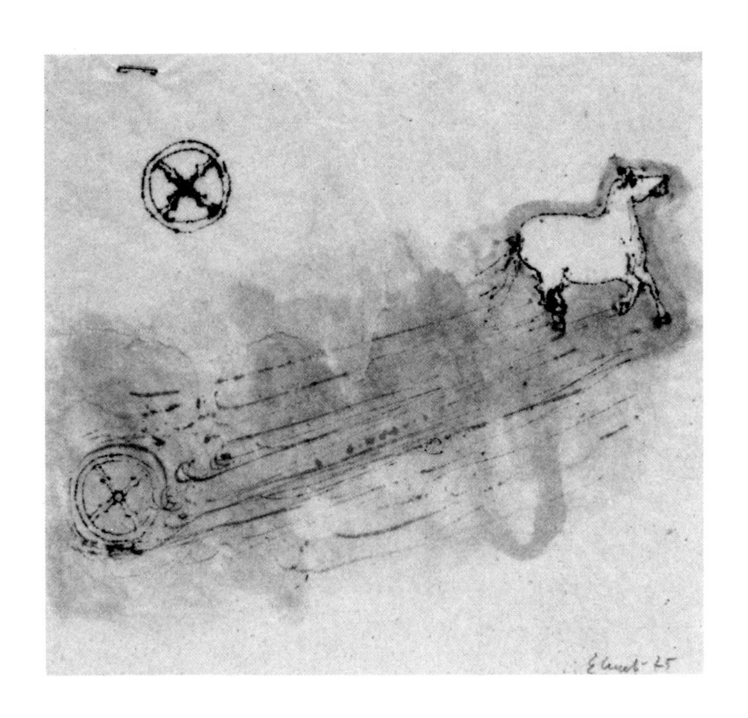

2. *Untitled*. 1975.

1976

3. *Bambino adulto*. 1976.

4. *Untitled*. 1976.

1977

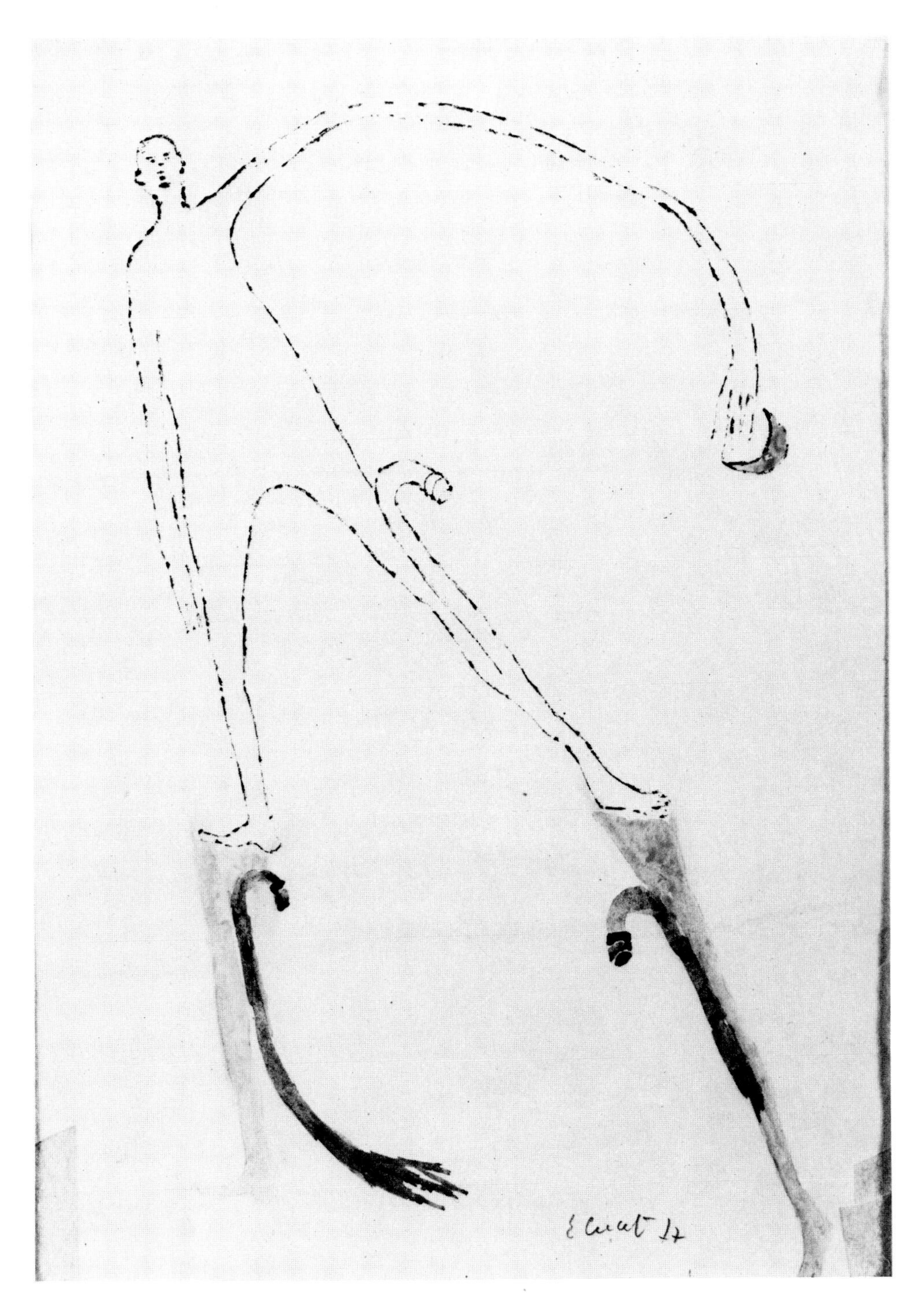

5. *Untitled*. 1977.

1978

6. *50 lire, un pesce in mano*. 1978.

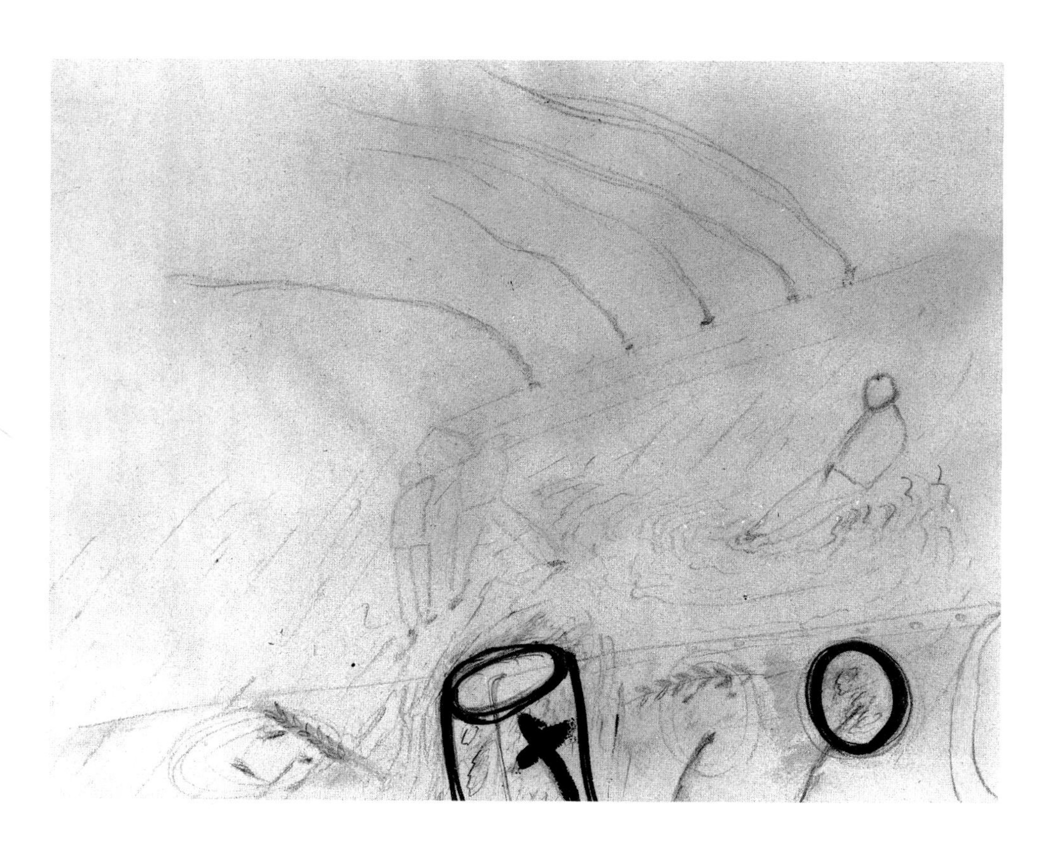

7. *Perché-anche-a-me*. 1978.

8. *Immagine Minore*. 1978.

9. *La cavalla azzurra*. 1978.

10. *La cavalla azzurra*. 1978.

11. *Untitled*. 1978.

12. *Tu e voi dove andate*. 1978.

13. *Vento di vino*. 1978.

14. *Portami a terra in un disegno*. 1978.

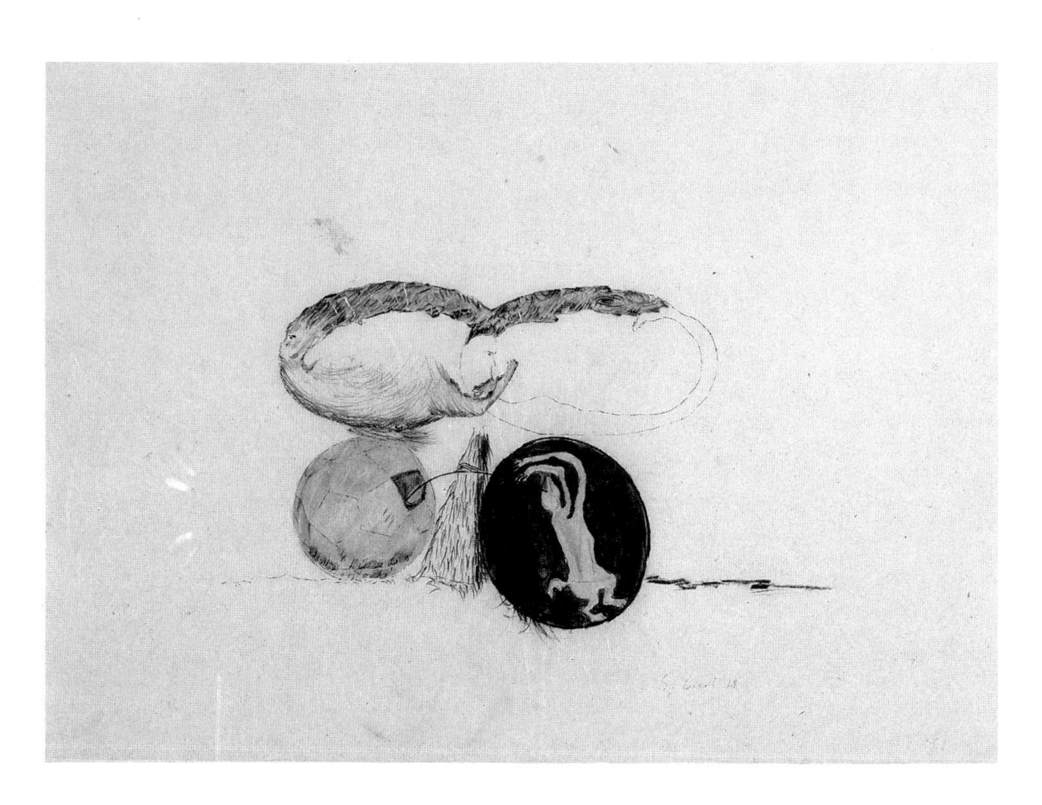

15. *Untitled*. 1978.

16. *Untitled (Per Achille)*. 1978-1979.

1979

17. *Vendemmia italiana*. 1979.

18. *Untitled*. 1979.

19. *Untitled*. 1979.

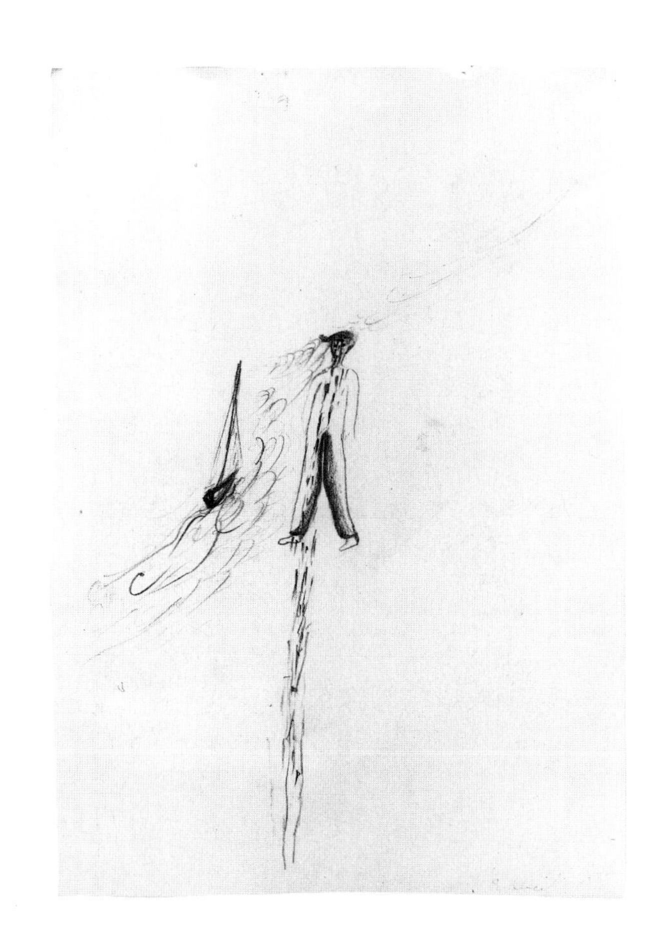

20. *Untitled*. 1979.

21. *Immagine minore italiana*. 1979.

22. *Untitled (Per Mercella)*. 1979.

23. *È fatto di pane*. 1979.

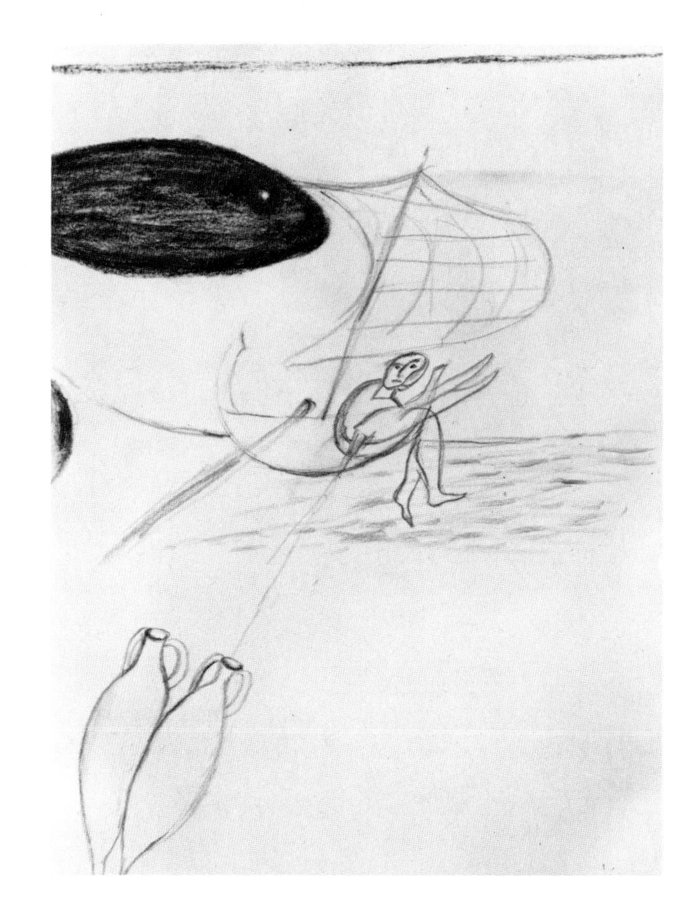

24. *Mare adriatico pesco*. 1979.

25. *Disegni marchigiani*. 1979.

26. *Untitled*. 1979.

27. *Non lo posso dire*. 1979.

28. *Campagna animalosa*. 1979.

29. *Tutti i disegni dell'Italia centrale*. 1979.

30. *Disegno al buio sul mare*. 1979.

31. *Adriatico! Mare disegnato per me*. 1979.

32. *Untitled*. 1979.

33. *La scopa dell'amore*. 1979.

34. *Ecclissi del sole*. 1979.

35. *Uomo del temporale*. 1979.

1980

36. *L'angelo*. 1980.

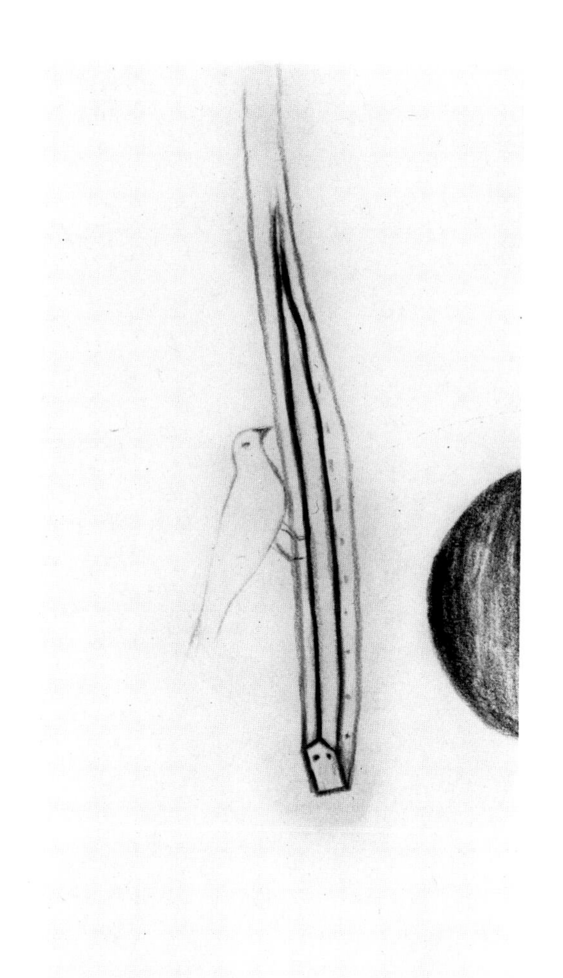

37. *La casa*. 1980.

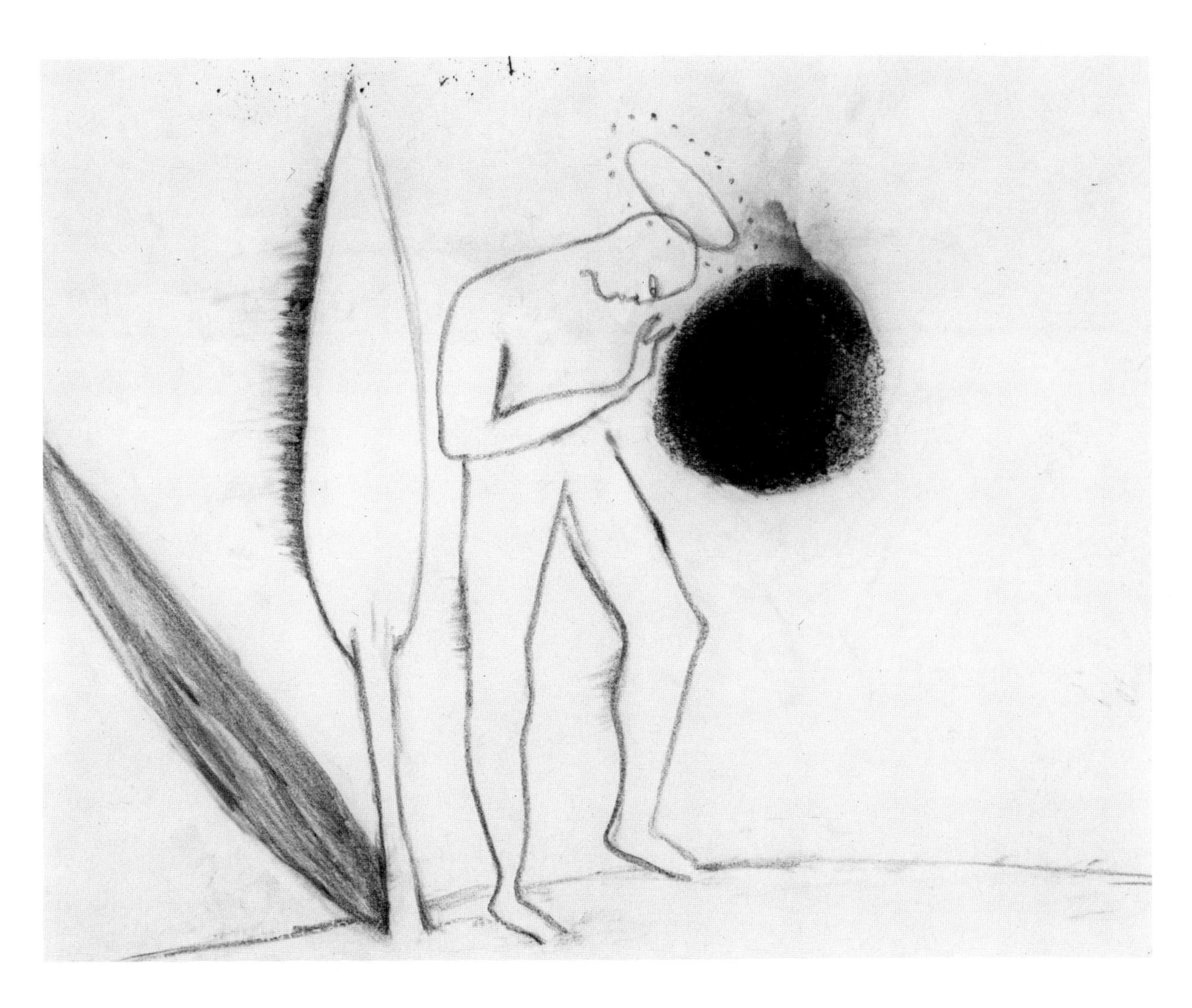

38. *Santo albero*. 1980.

39. *Palla-santa*. 1980.

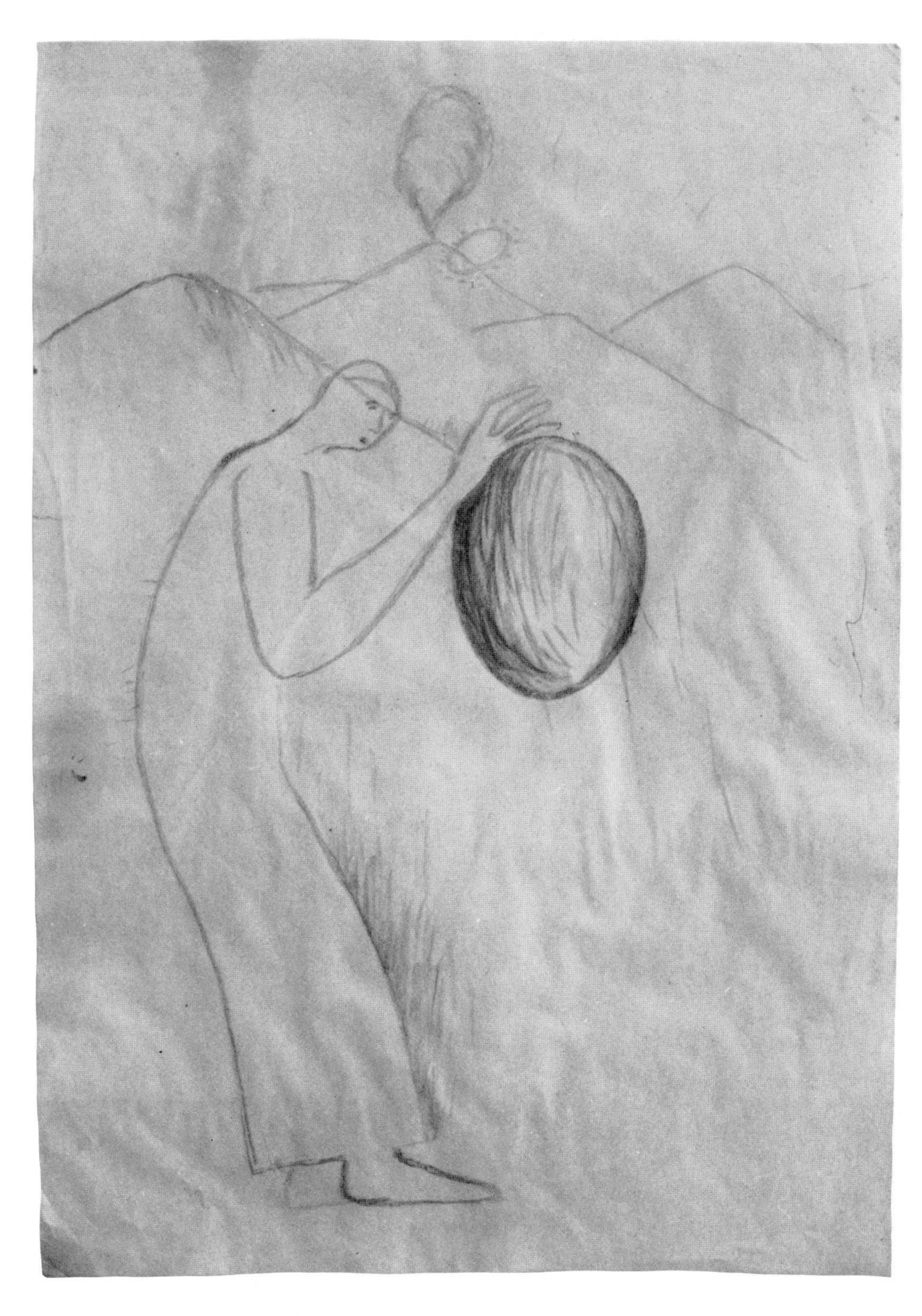

40. *Disegno minore marchigiano*. 1980.

41. *Untitled*. 1980.

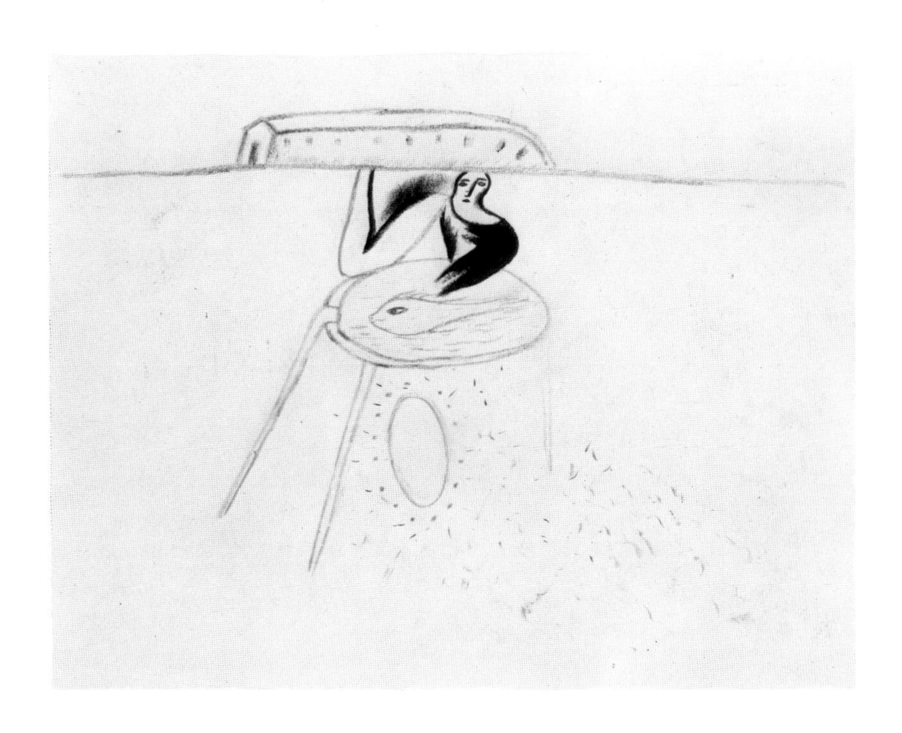

42. *Pesci santi da Ancona*. 1980.

43. *Al buio sul mare adriatico*. 1980.

44. *Tutte le montagne sono sante*. 1980.

45. *Immagine minore marchigiana*. 1980.

46. *Il santo di Loreto*. 1980.

47. *Tutti i pesci devono andare piano*. 1980.

48. *Disegno feroce di 1980*. 1980.

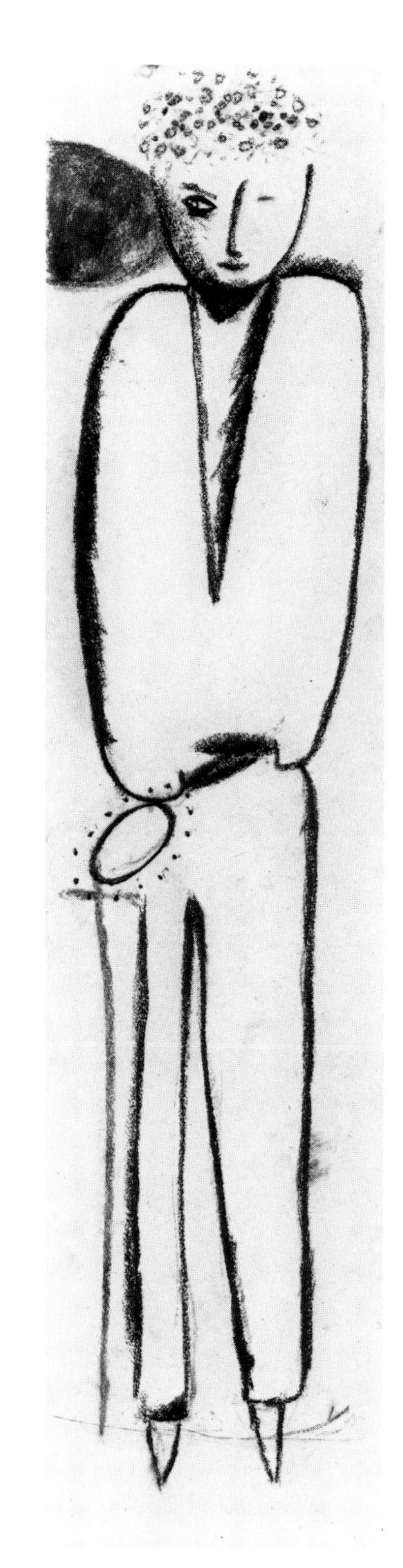

49. *Untitled*. 1980.

50. *5 Monti sono santi*. 1980.

1981

51. *Fontana innamorata*. 1981.

52. *Preghiera del'arbero*. 1981.

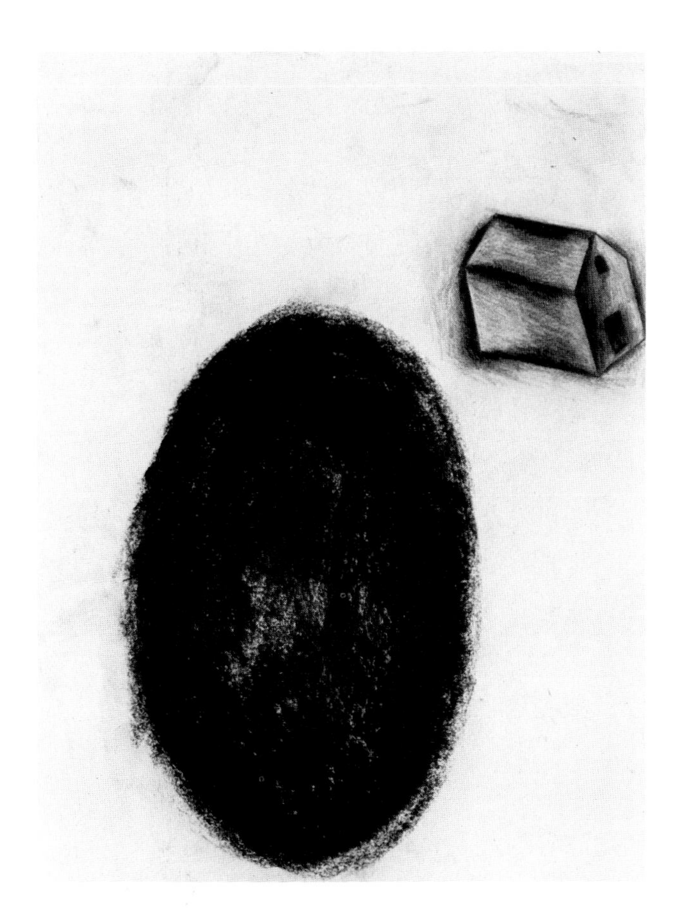

53. *Casa terrestre*. 1981.

54. *Miracolo di legno*. 1981.

55. *Il santo delle tempeste*. 1981.

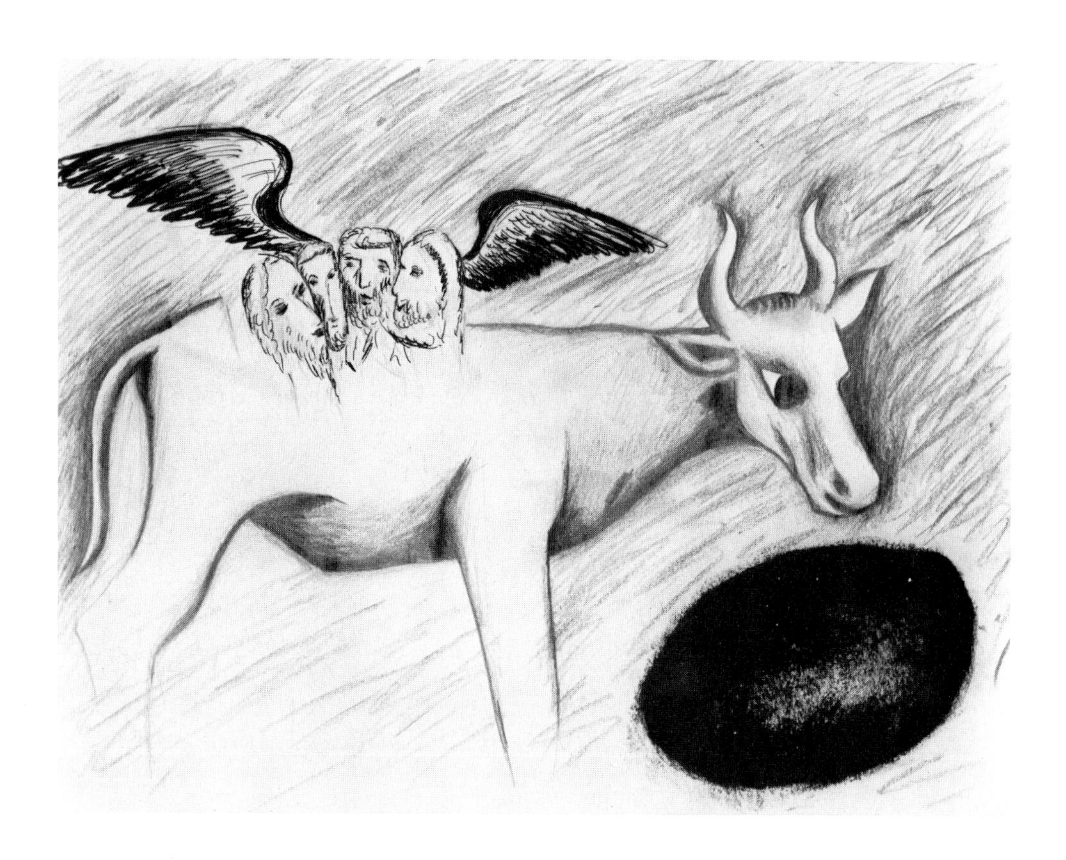

56. *Trasporto angelico*. 1981.

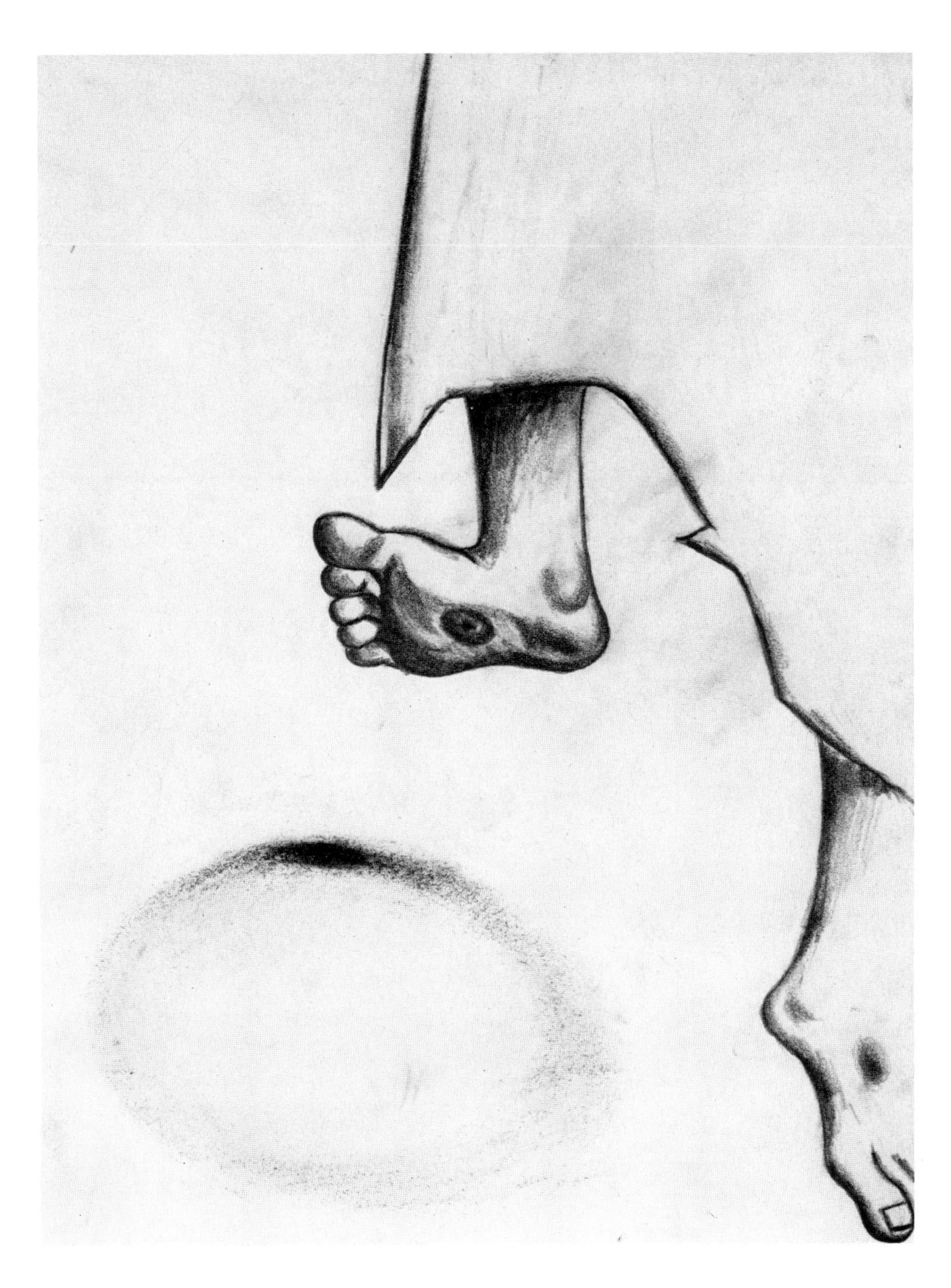

57. *Santo, santo*. 1981.

58. *Untitled*. 1981.

59. *Untitled*. 1981.

60. *Untitled*. 1981.

61. *Untitled*. 1981.

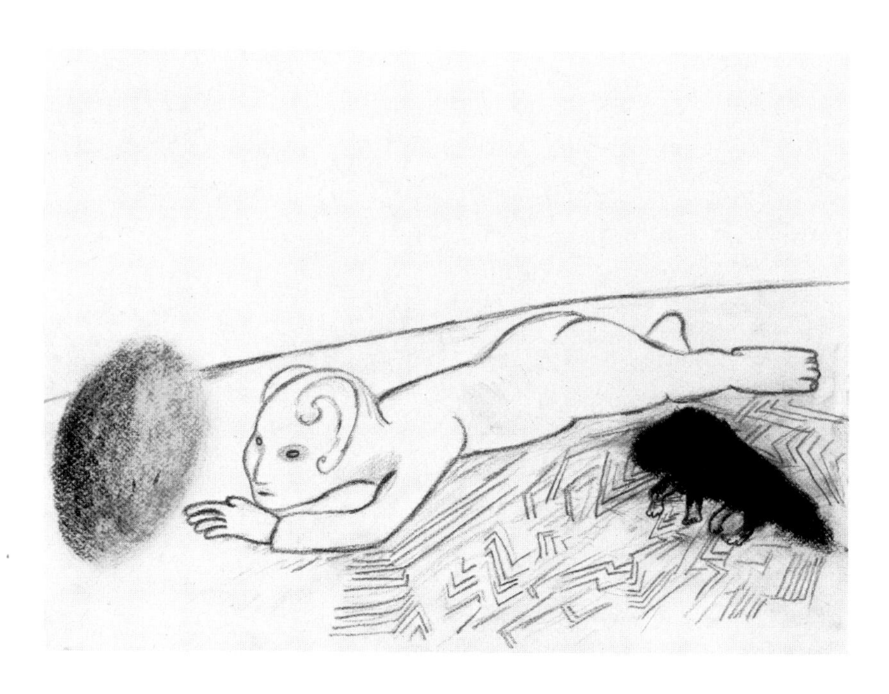

62. *Untitled*. 1981.

63. *Untitled*. 1981.

64. *Untitled*. 1981.

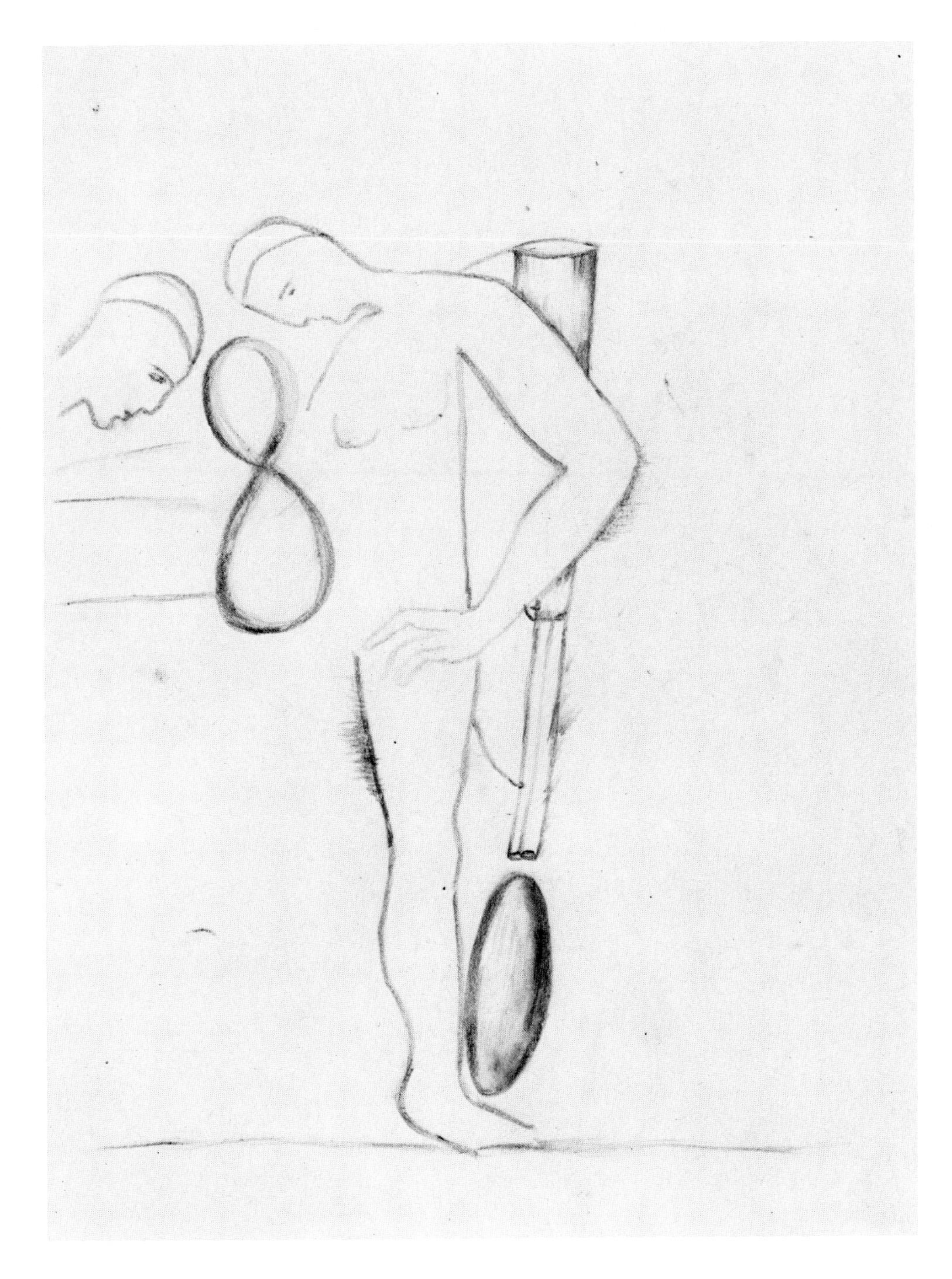

65. *Untitled*. 1981.

66. *Il vento delle pietre*. 1981.

67. *I fiori de pietra*. 1981.

68. *Untitled*. 1981.

69. *Miracolo*. 1981.

70. *La pietra del tempo*. 1981.

71. *Il miracolo delle montagne*. 1981.

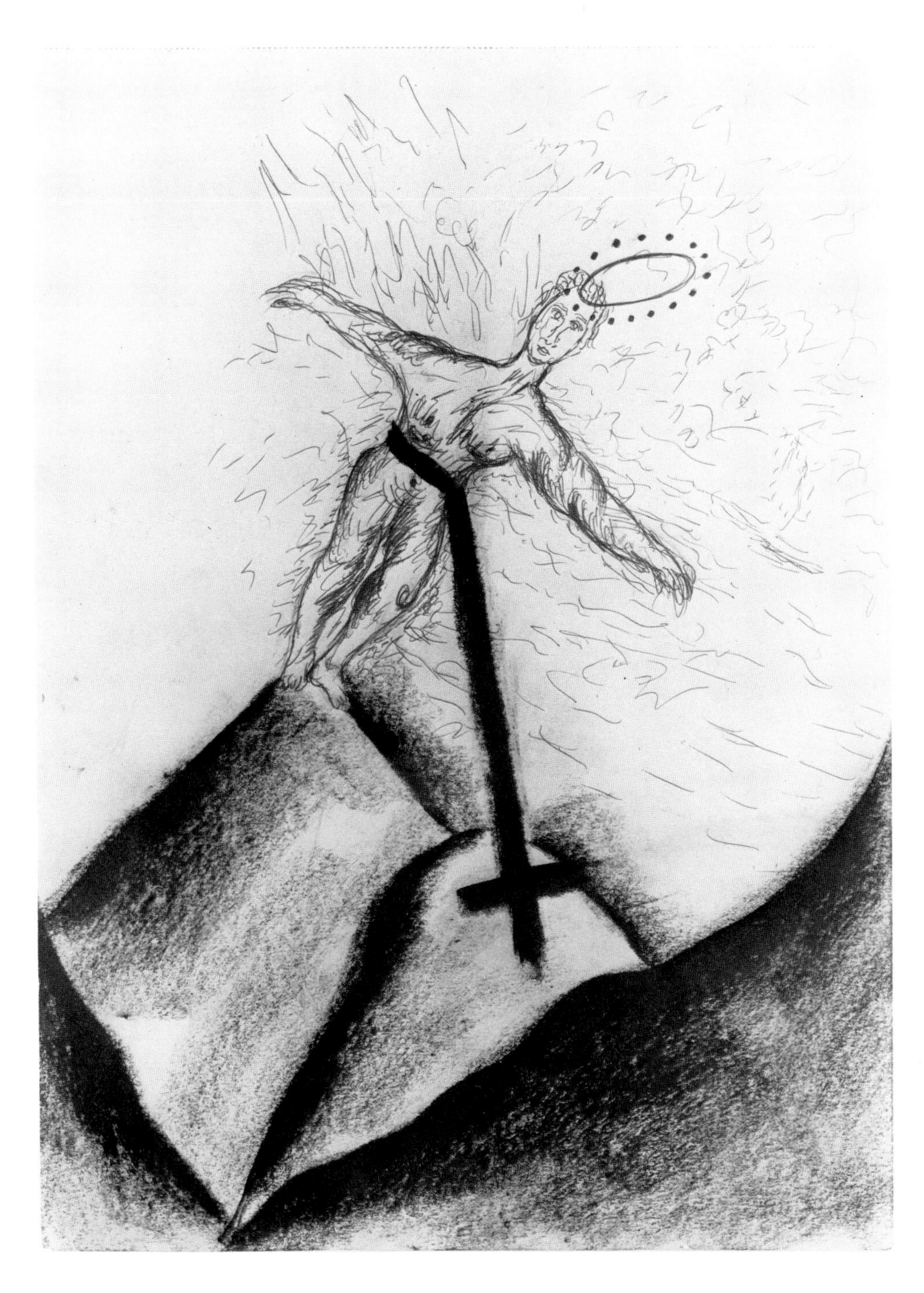

72. *El miracolo delle montagne*. 1981.

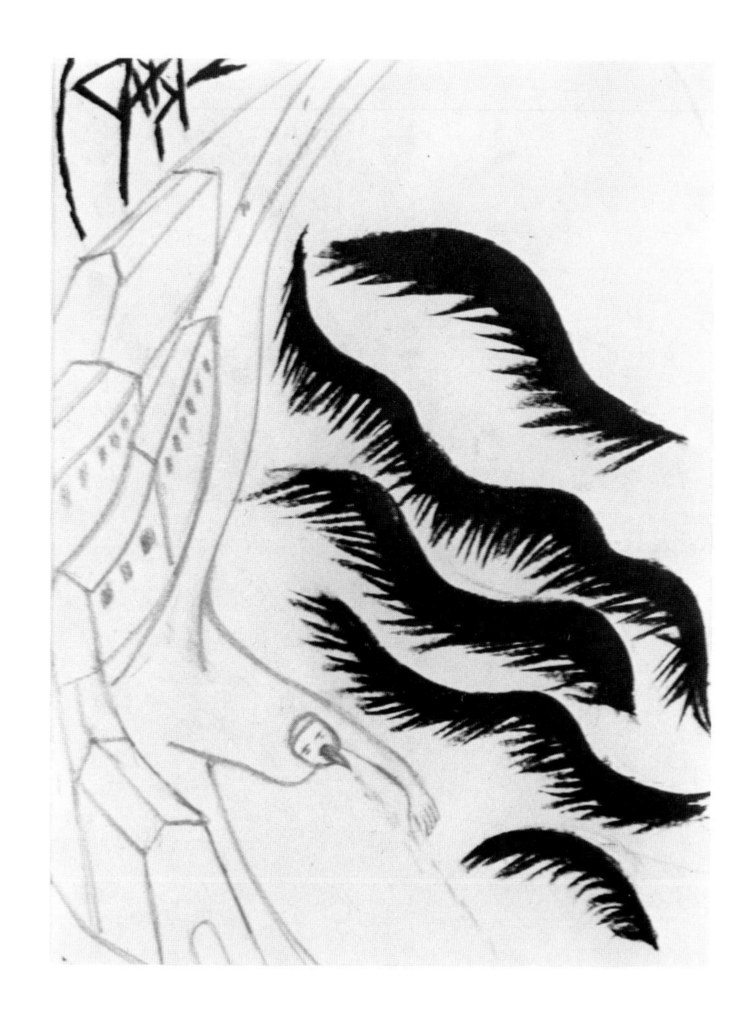

73. *Le case vanno in discesa*. 1981.

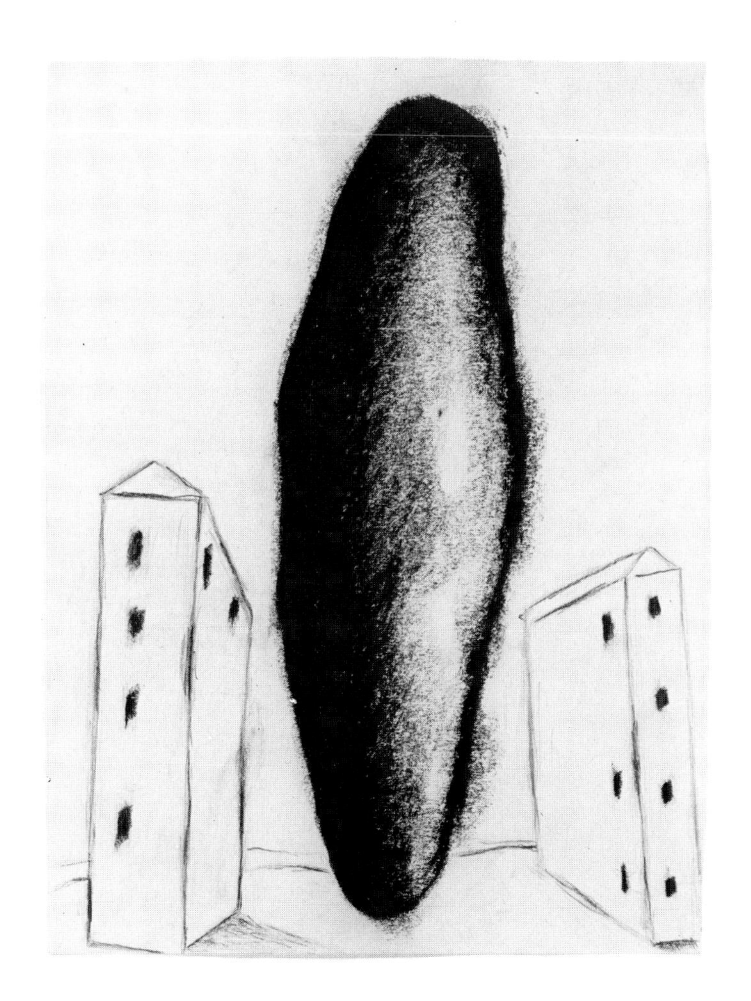

74. *Pane santo*. 1981.

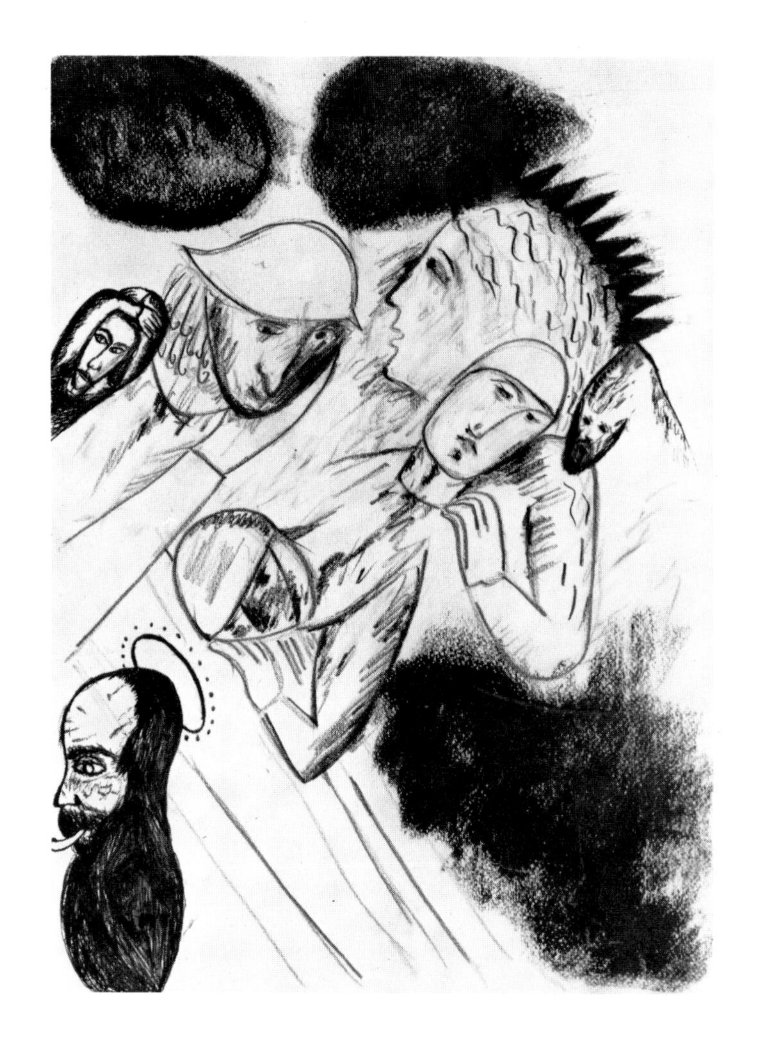

75. *I peccati dei sassi.* 1981.

76. *Untitled*. Around 1981.

77. *Il sentimento di un eroe*. 1981.

78. *Per la mia fede*. 1981.

79. *Untitled*. 1981.

1982

80. *Tesoro misterioso*. 1982.

81. *Le case si riempiono in cielo*. 1982.

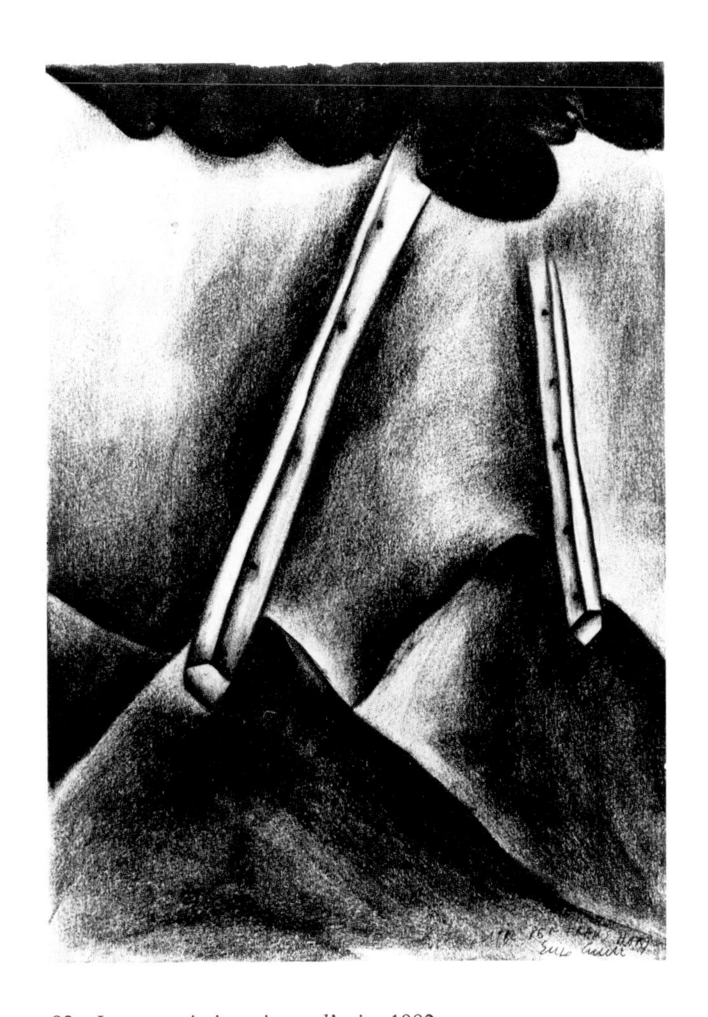

82. *Le case si riempiono d'aria*. 1982.

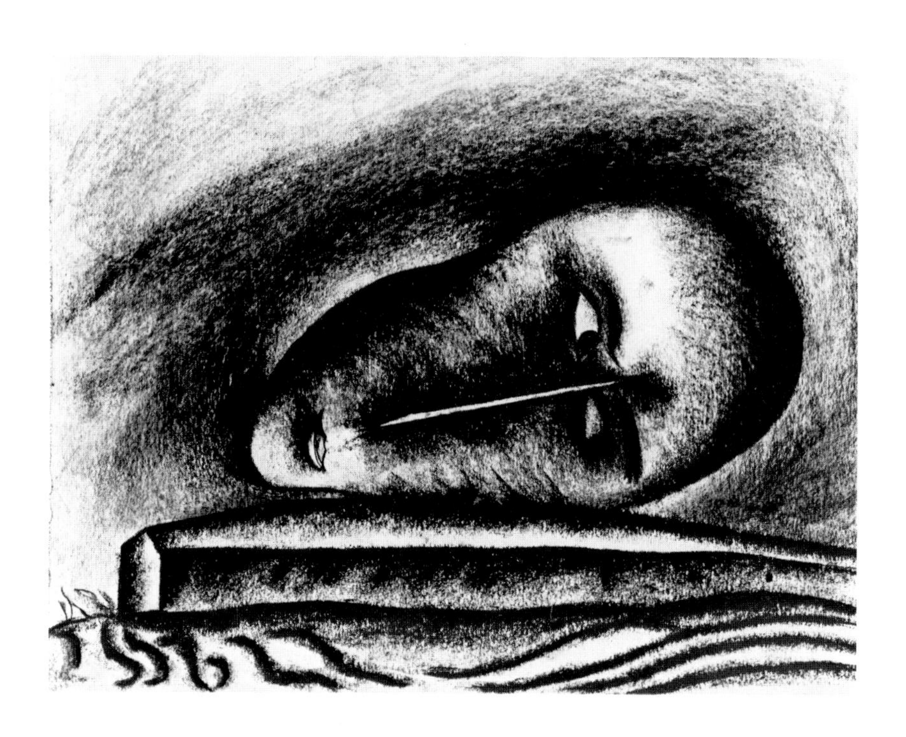

83. *Il pensiero della casa*. 1982.

84. *La casa cae sogna*. 1982.

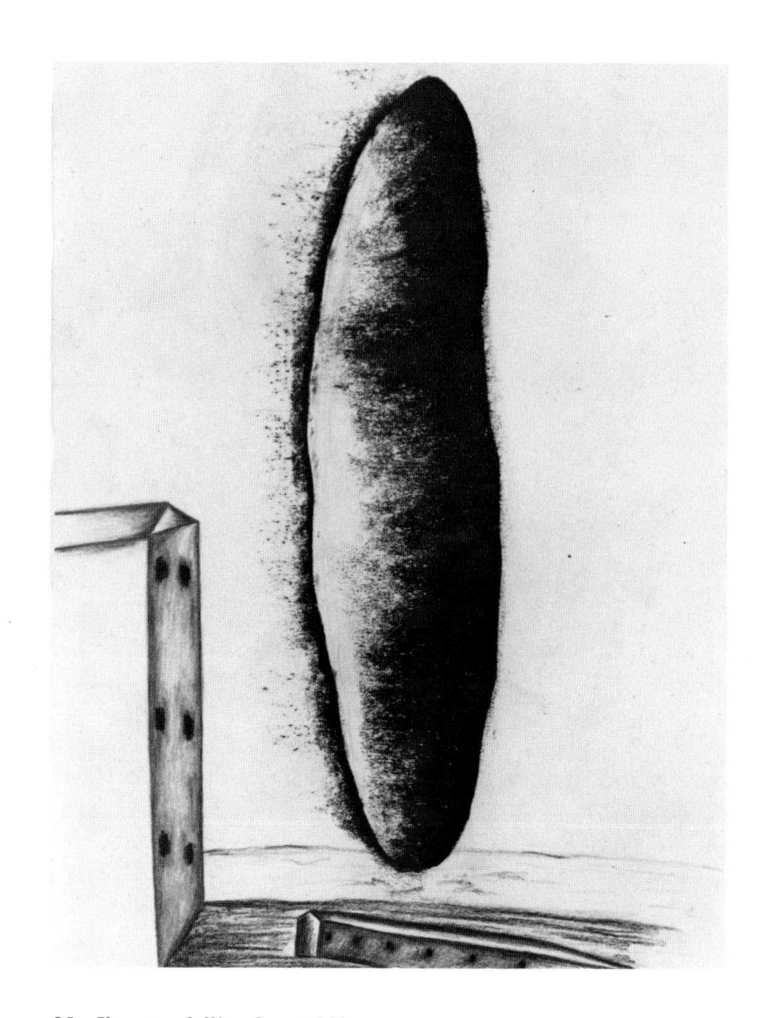

85. *Il parto dell'ombra*. 1982.

86. *Il respiro della battaglia*. 1982.

87. *L'anima nel paesaggio*. 1982.

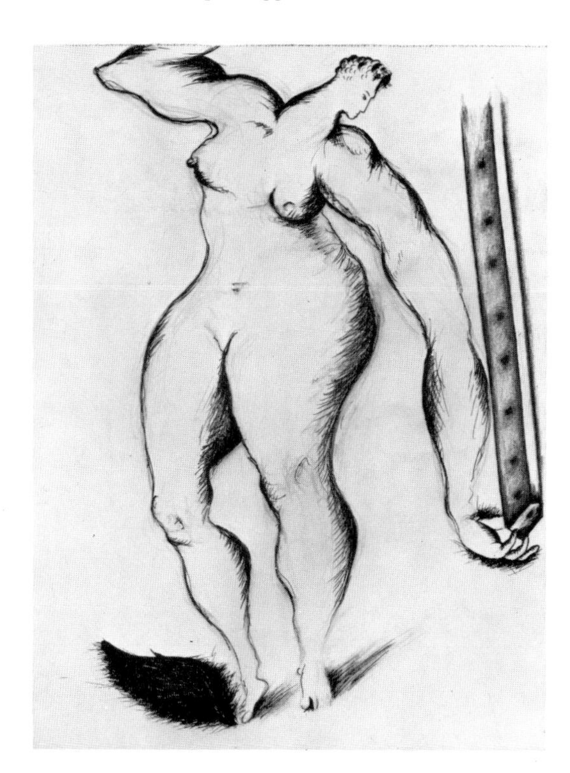

88. *Viaggio della santa casa*. 1982.

89. *Die Berge widerstehen den Tieren*. 1982.

90. *Untitled*. 1982.

91. *Il sogno di un giorno*. 1981-1982.

92. *Passeggiata della morte*. 1982.

93. *Un sogno ritrovato*, 1982.

1983

94. *Untitled*. 1983.

95. *Kolosseum zu: Giulio Cesare Roma*. 1983.

96. *Giulio Cesare Roma*. 1983.

97. *La vita è spaventata*. 1983.

98. *I pensieri arrivano ancora*. 1983.

99. *Il ritratto di un pensiero*. 1983.

100. *Dei ed eroi*. 1983.

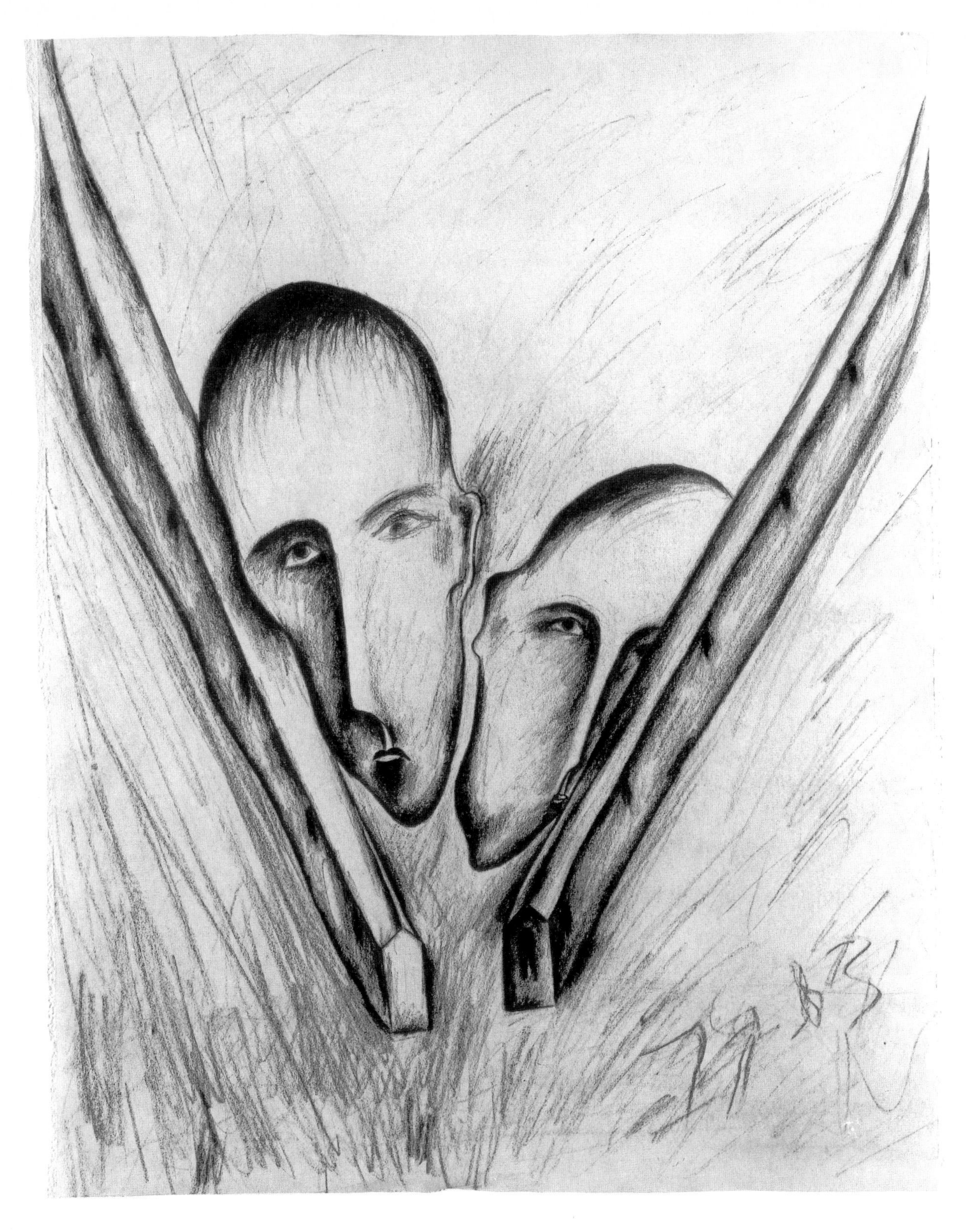

101. *Untitled*. 1983.

102. *Untitled*. 1983.

103. *Untitled*. 1983.

104. *Untitled*. 1983.

105. *Circostanza*. 1983.

106. *Paesaggio barbaro*. 1983.

107. *Più vicino agli dei*. 1983.

108. *Sperone*. 1983.

109. *Uno scherzo della natura*. 1983.

110. *Il sogno del mare*. 1983.

111. *Untitled*. 1983.

112. *Il desiderio di un paesaggio*. 1983.

113. *Pasto cosmico*. 1983.

114. *Accanto allo spirito degli eroi.* 1983.

115. *La fisarmonica della terra*. 1983.

116. *La ninna nanna della terra*. 1983.

117. *Untitled*. 1983.

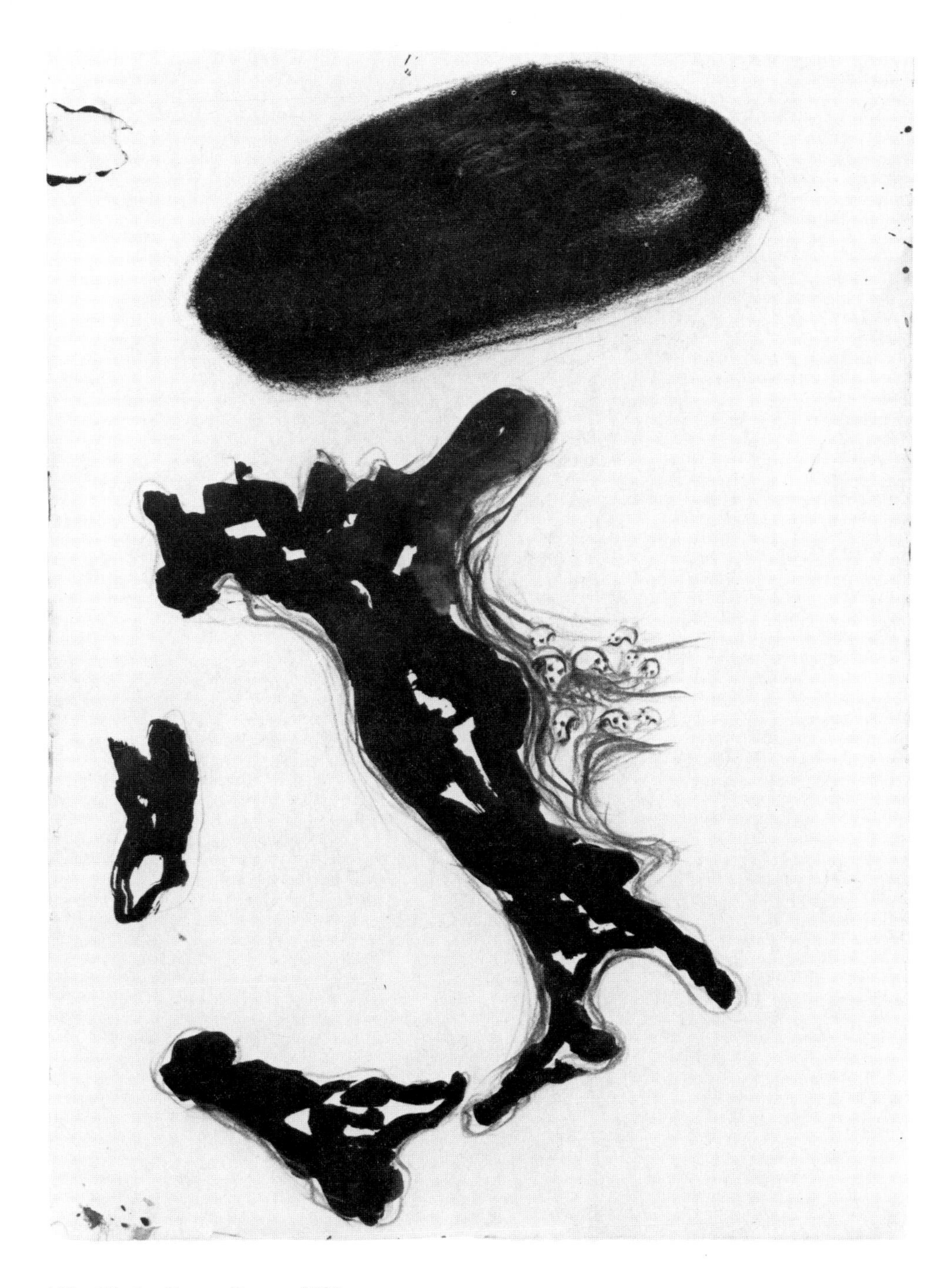

118. *Giulio Cesare Roma*. 1983.

119. *Untitled*. 1983.

120. *Untitled*. 1983.

121. *Untitled*. 1983.

122. *Untitled*. 1983.

123. *Girotondo della vita*. 1983.

124. *Untitled*. 1983.

125. *Giulio Cesare Roma*. 1983.

126. *Untitled*. 1983.

127. *Gli alberi respirano con gli animali.* 1983.

1984

128. *Untitled*. 1984.

129. *Untitled*. 1984.

130. *Untitled*. 1984.

131. *Untitled*. 1984.

132. *Untitled*. 1984.

133. *Pesce predicatore*. 1984.

134. *La casa gravida*. 1984.

135. *Untitled*. 1984.

136. *Untitled*. 1984.

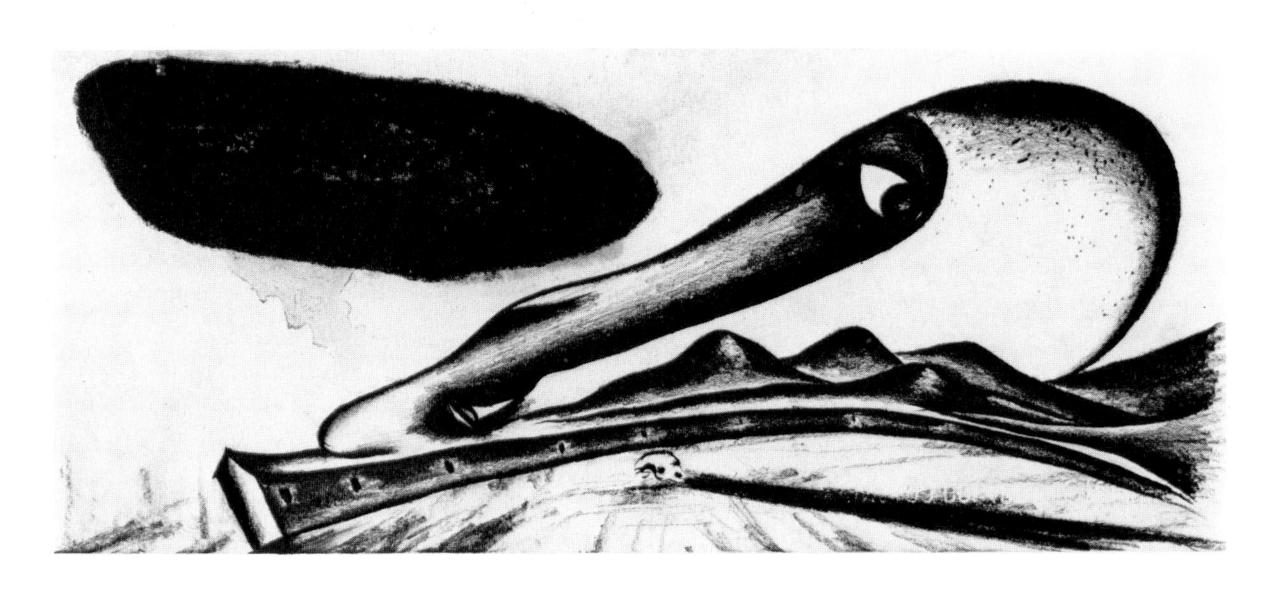

137. *Ultimo eroe*. 1984.

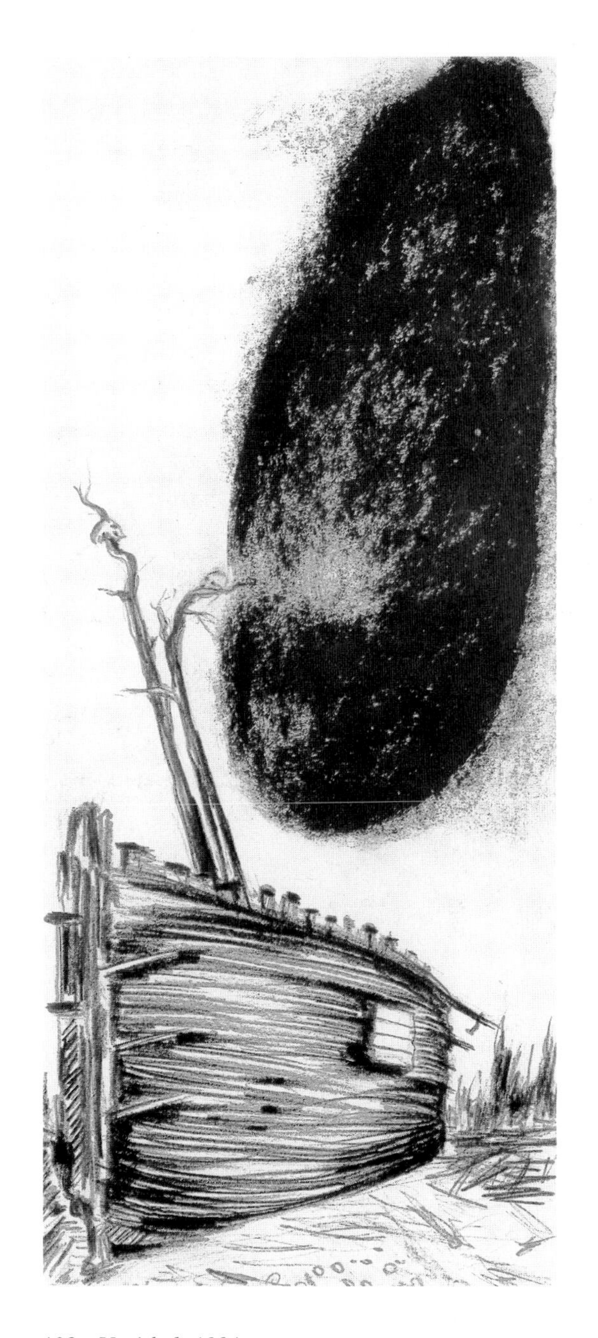

138. *Untitled*. 1984.

139. *Untitled*. 1984.

140. *Untitled (Vitebsk-Harar)*. 1984.

141. *Vitebsk-Harar*. 1984.

142. *Untitled (Vitebsk-Harar)*. 1984.

143. *Harar*. 1984.

144. *Vitebsk-Harar*. 1984.

145. *Untitled (Vitebsk-Harar)*. 1984.

146. *Untitled (Vitebsk-Harar)*. 1984.

147. *Untitled*. 1984.

148. *Il veleno delle sculture*. 1984.

149. *Il veleno delle sculture*. 1984.

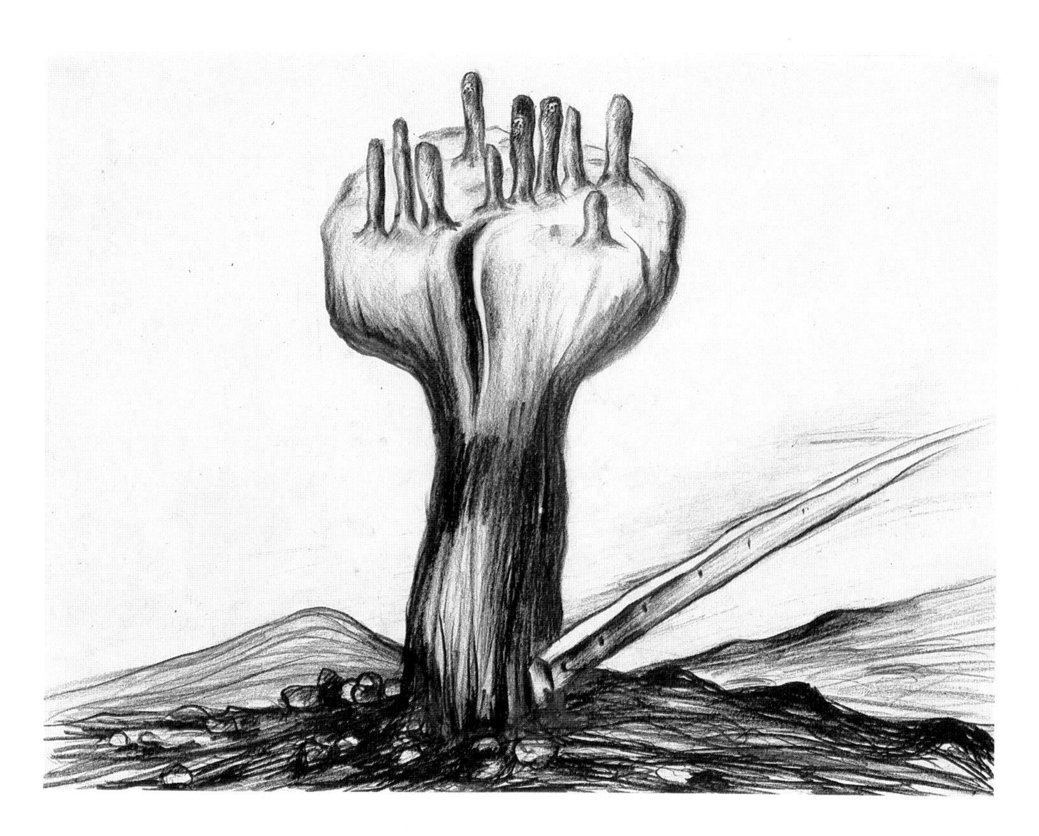

150. *Untitled*. 1984.

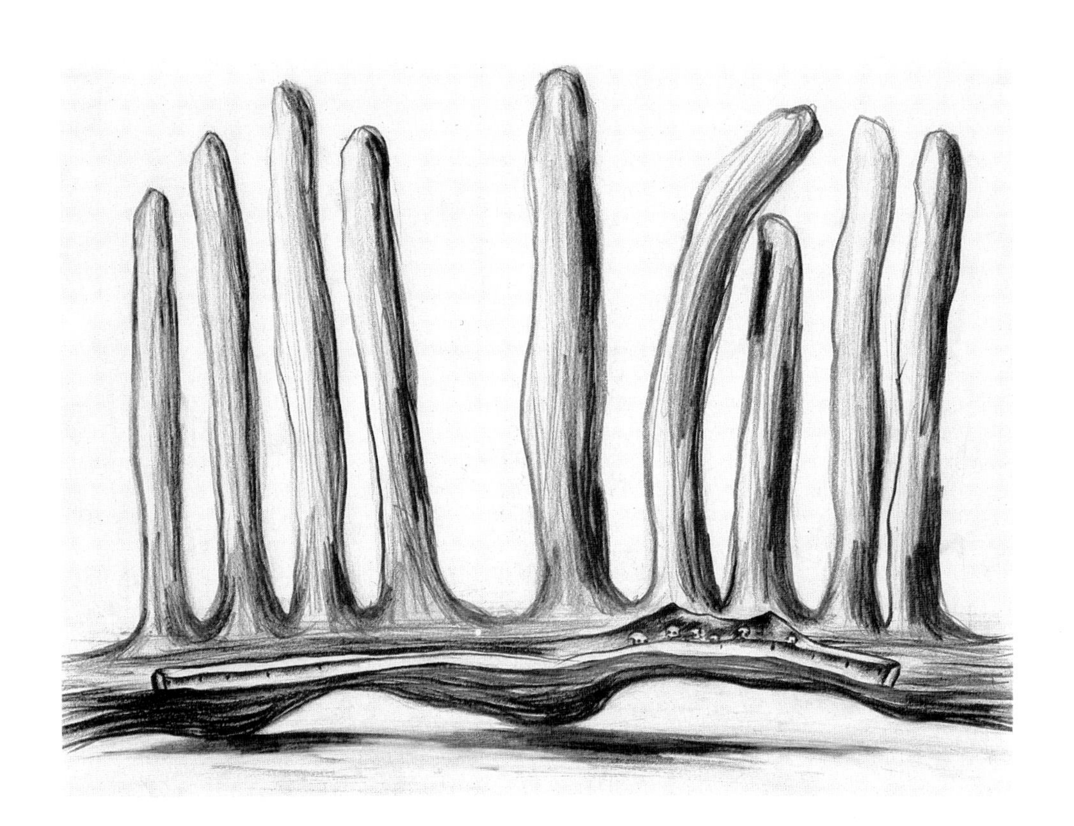

151. *Untitled*. 1984.

152. *Untitled*. 1984.

153. *Untitled*. 1984.

154. *Untitled*. 1984.

155. *Untitled*. 1984.

156. *Untitled*. 1984.

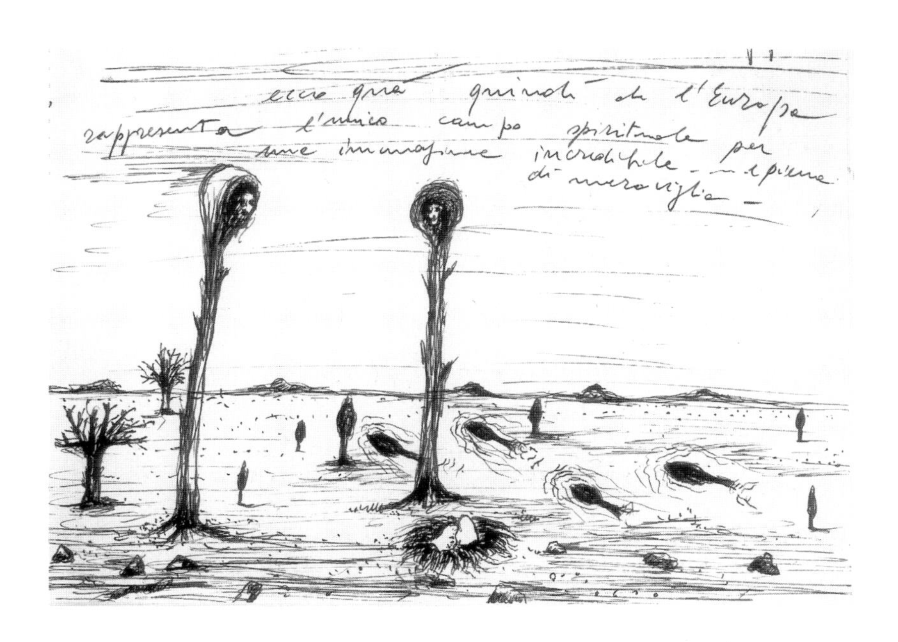

157. *Untitled*. 1984.

1985

158. *Untitled*. 1985.

159. *Untitled*. 1984-1985.

160. *Untitled*. 1984-1985.

161. *Untitled*. 1984-1985.

162. *Untitled*. 1984-1985.

163. *Untitled*. 1985.

164. *Untitled*. 1984-1985.

165. *Untitled*. 1984-1985.

166. *Untitled*. 1984-1985.

167. *Untitled*. 1984-1985.

168. *Untitled*. 1984-1985.

169. *Untitled*. 1984-1985.

170. *Untitled*. 1984-1985.

171. *Untitled*. 1984-1985.

172. *Untitled*. 1984-1985.

173. *Untitled*. 1984-1985.

174. *Untitled*. 1985.

175. *Untitled*. 1985.

176. *Untitled*. 1984-1985.

177. *Untitled*. 1984-1985.

178. *Untitled*. 1985.

179. *Untitled*. 1984-1985.

180. *Untitled*. 1985.

181. *Untitled*. 1985.

182. *Untitled*. 1984-1985.

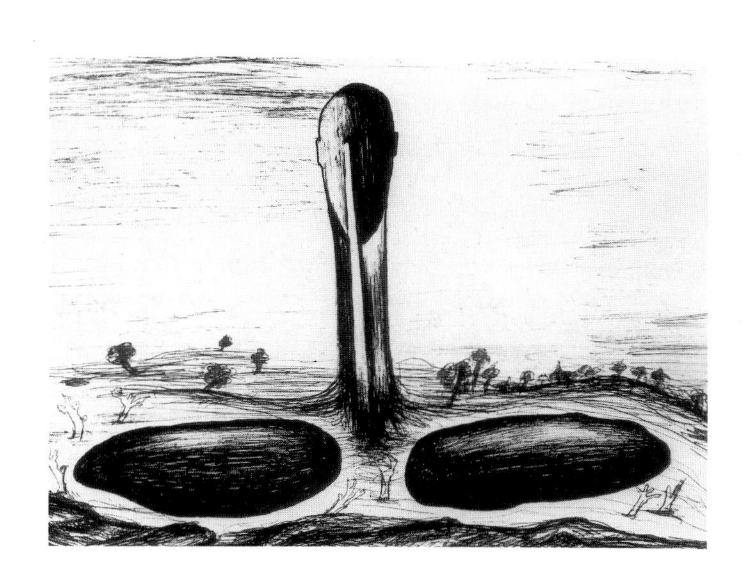

183. *Untitled*. 1984-1985.

184. *Untitled*. 1985.

185. *Untitled*. 1985.

186. *Untitled*. 1985.

187. *Untitled*. 1985.

188. *Untitled*. 1985.

189. *Untitled*. 1985.

190. *Untitled*. 1985.

191. *Untitled*. 1985.

192. *Untitled*. 1985.

193. *Untitled*. 1985.

194. *Untitled*. 1985.

195. *Untitled*. 1985.

196. *Untitled*. 1985.

197. *Untitled*. 1985.

198. *Harar, A.R.* 1985.

199. *Untitled*. 1985.

200. *Untitled* (Solchi d'Europa). 1985.

201. *Untitled*. 1985.

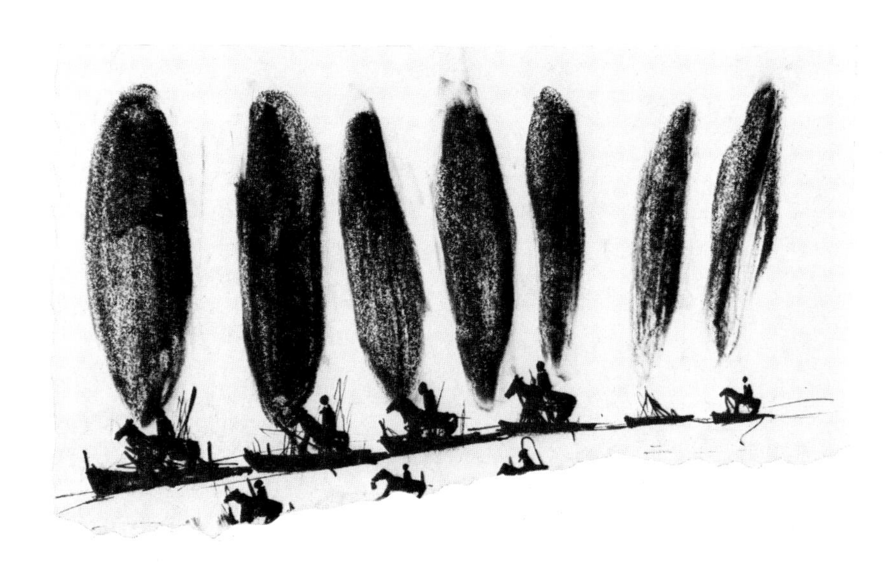

202. *Untitled*. 1985.

203. *Untitled*. 1985.

204. *Harar*. 1985.

205. *Harar, A.R.* 1985.

206. *La stanza del fiato*. 1985.

207. *Untitled*. 1985.

208. *Untitled*. 1985.

209. *Untitled*. 1985.

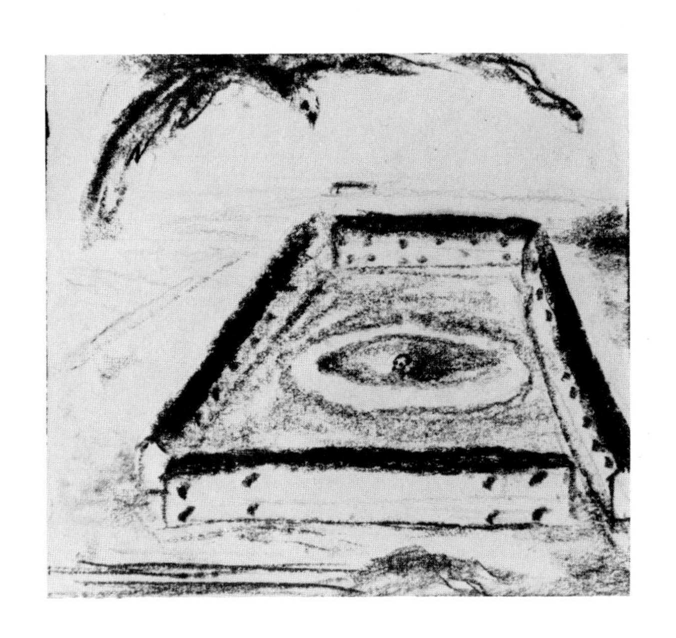

210. *Untitled*. 1985.

211. *Untitled*. 1985.

212. *Untitled*. 1985.

213. *Untitled*. 1985.

214. *Untitled*. 1985.

215. *Untitled*. 1985.

1986

216. *Untitled*. 1986.

217. *Untitled*. 1986.

218. *Untitled*. 1986.

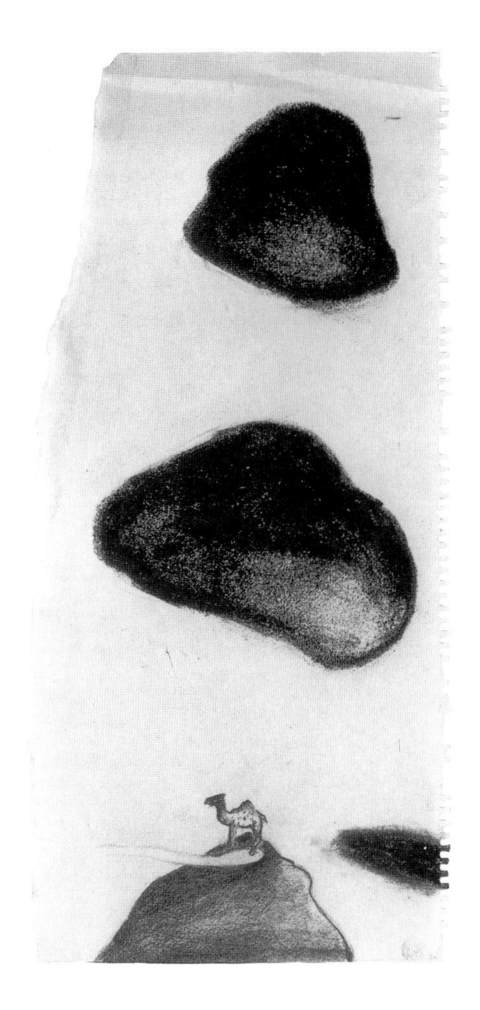

219. *Untitled*. 1986.

220. *Untitled*. 1986.

221. *Untitled*. 1986.

222. *Untitled*. 1986.

223. *Untitled*. 1986.

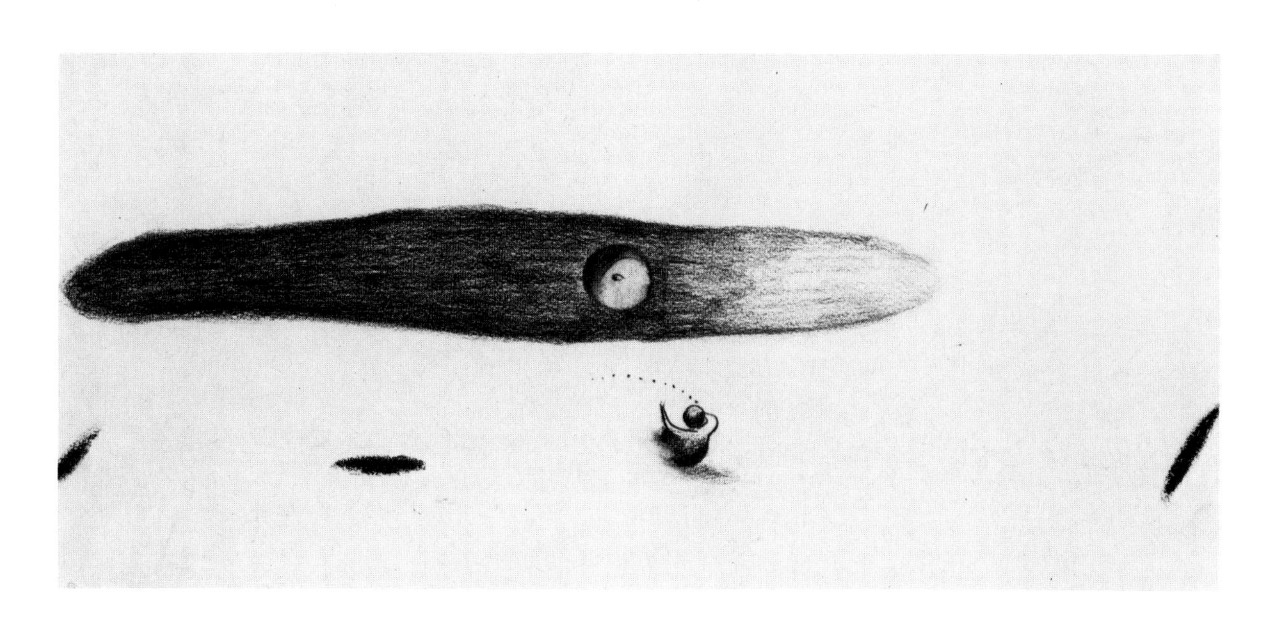

224. *Untitled*. 1986.

225. *Untitled*. 1986.

226. *Untitled*. 1986.

227. *Untitled*. 1986.

228. *Untitled*. 1986.

229. *Untitled*. 1986.

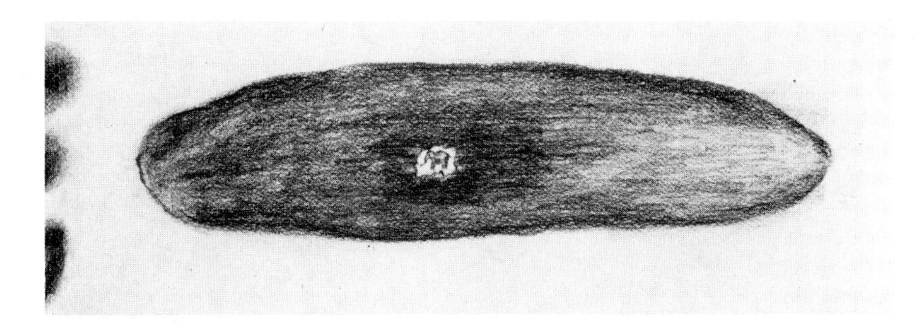

230. *Untitled*. 1986.

231. *Untitled*. 1986.

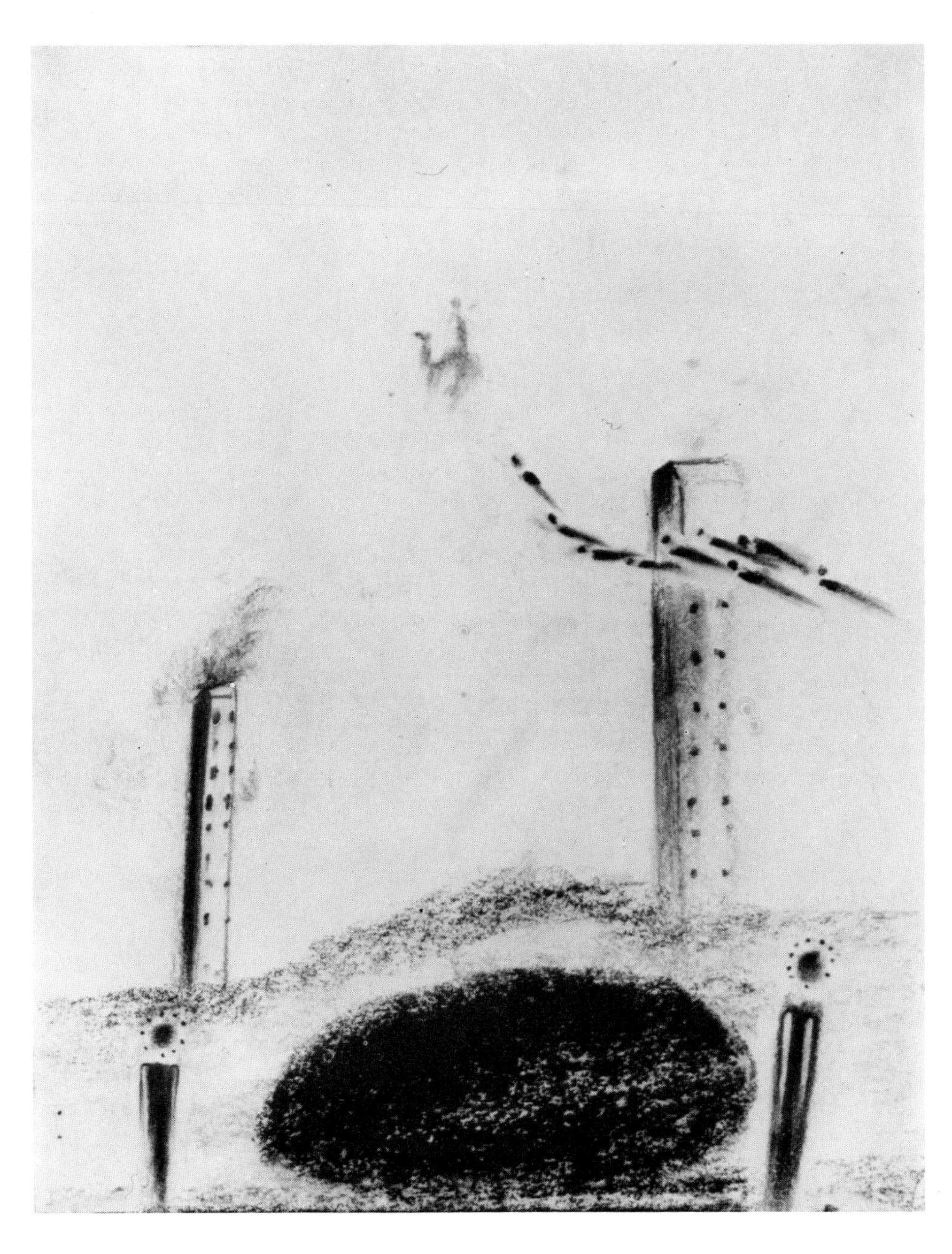

232. *Untitled*. 1986.

233. *Untitled*. 1986.

234. *Untitled*. 1986.

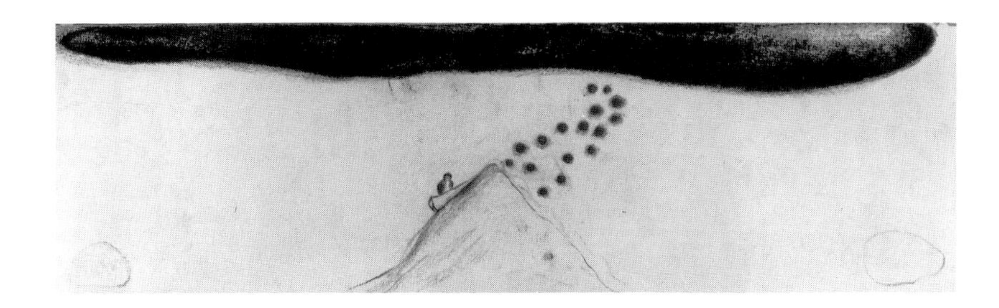

235. *Untitled*. 1986.

236. *Untitled*. 1986.

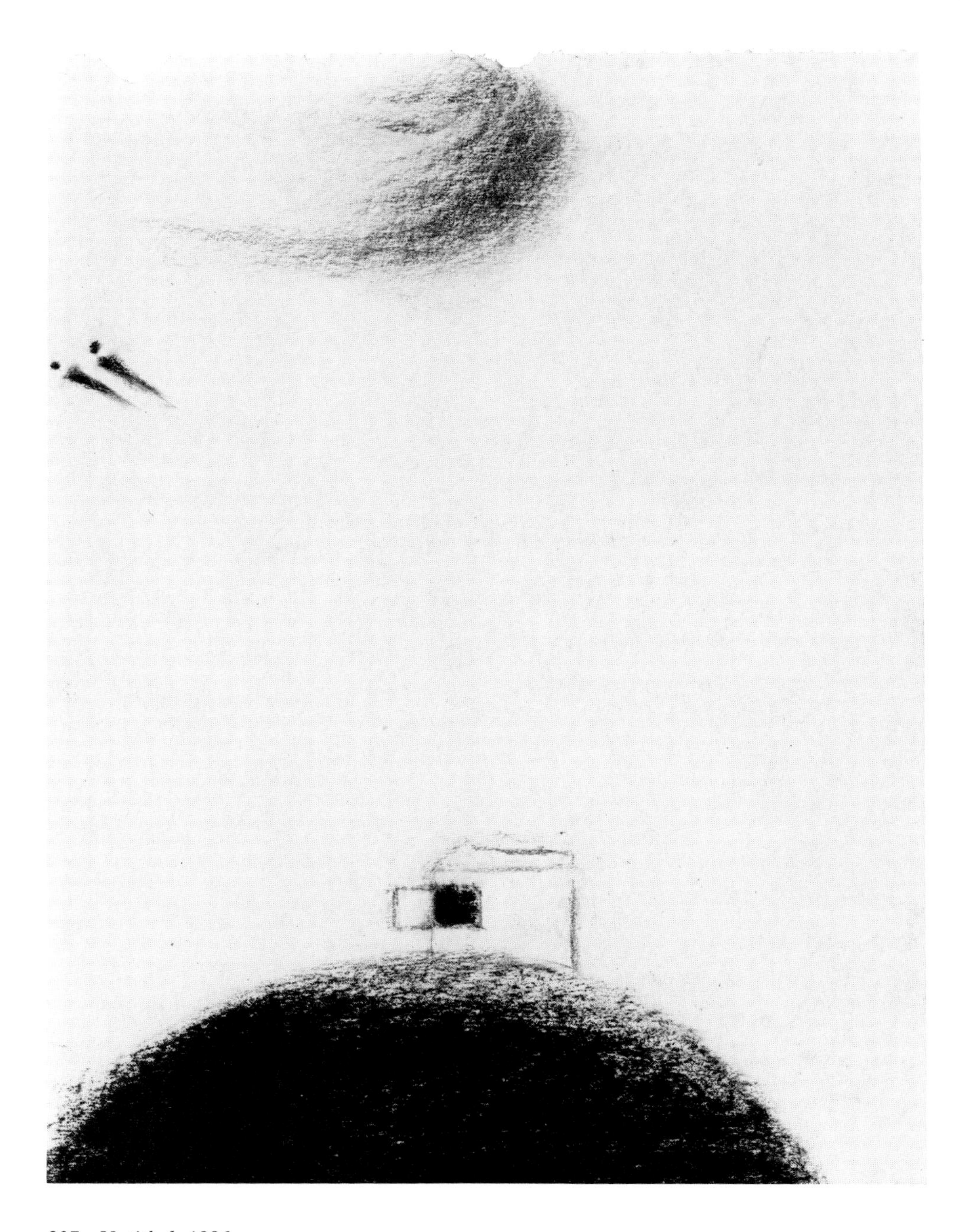

237. *Untitled*. 1986.

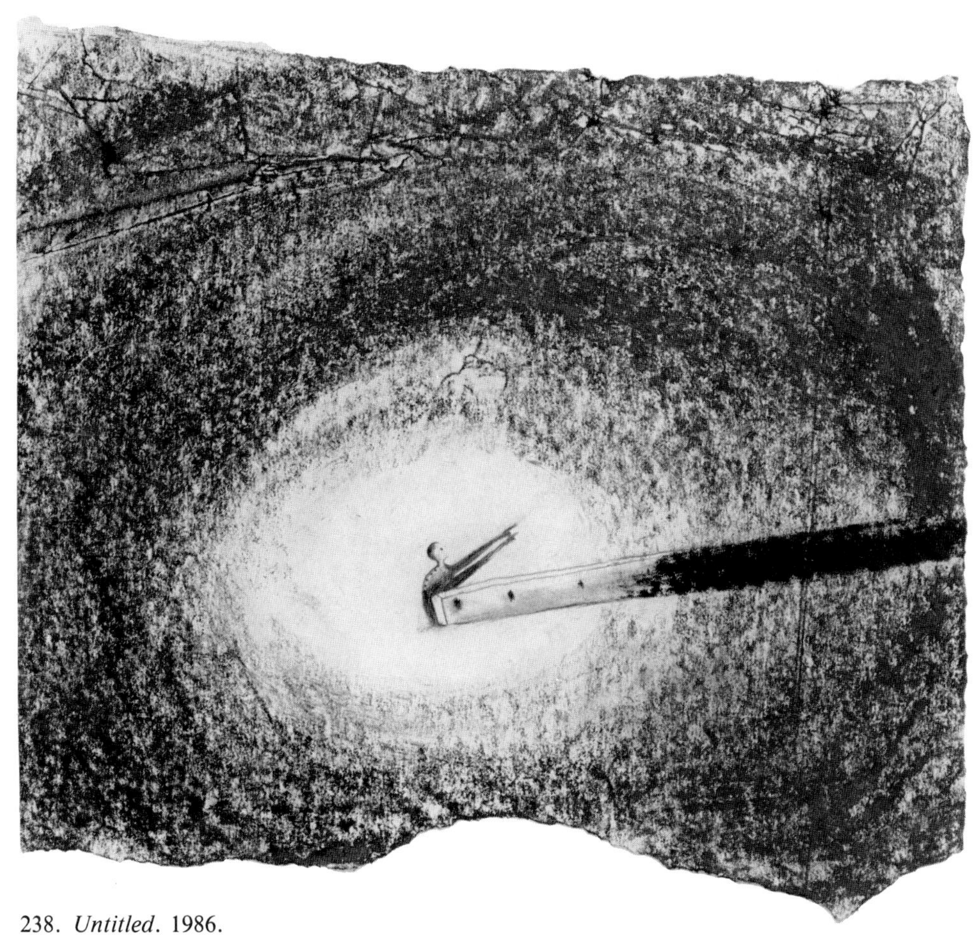

238. *Untitled*. 1986.

239. *Untitled*. 1986.

240. *Untitled*. 1986.

241. *Untitled*. 1986.

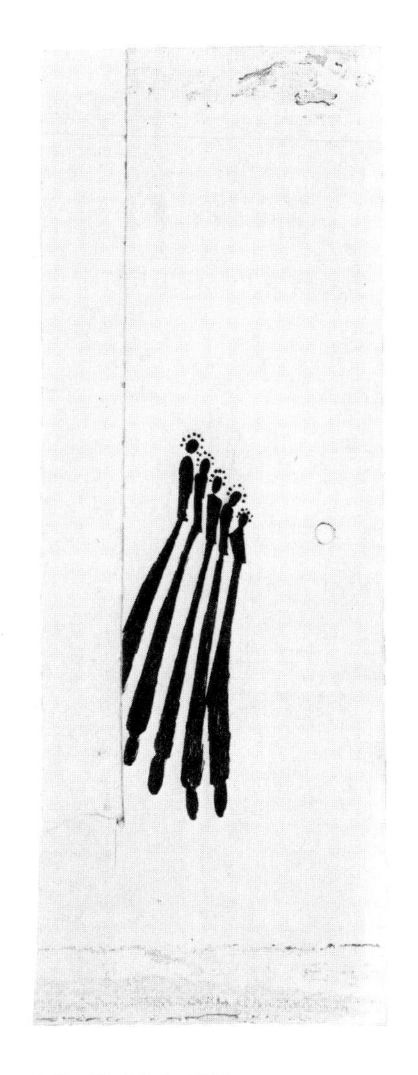

242. *Untitled*. 1986.

243. *Untitled*. 1986.

244. *Untitled*. 1986.

245. *Untitled*. 1986.

246. *Untitled*. 1986.

247. *Untitled*. 1986.

248. *Untitled*. 1986.

249. *Untitled*. 1986.

250. *Untitled*. 1986.

251. *Untitled*. 1986.

252. *Untitled*. 1986.

1987

253. *Untitled*. 1987.

254. *Untitled*. 1987.

255. *Untitled*. 1987.

256. *Untitled*. 1987.

257. *Untitled*. 1987.

258. *Untitled*. 1987.

259. *Untitled*. 1987.

260. *Untitled*. 1987.

261. *Untitled*. 1987.

262. *Untitled*. 1987.

263. *Untitled*. 1987.

264. *Untitled*. 1987.

265. *Untitled*. 1987.

266. *Untitled*. 1987.

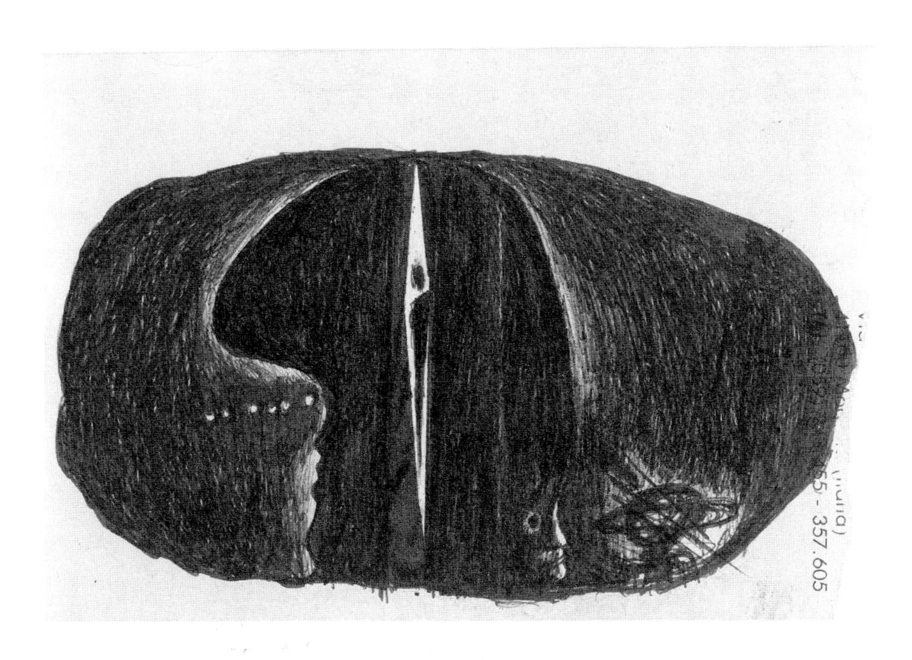

267. *Untitled*. 1987.

268. *Untitled*. 1987.

269. *Untitled*. 1987.

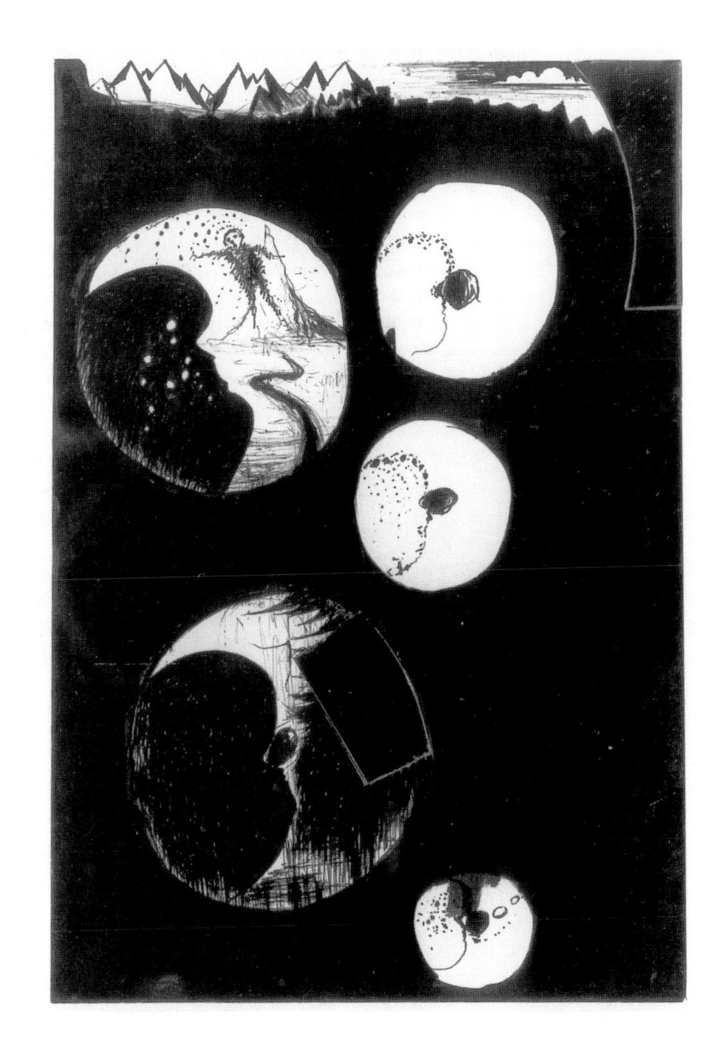

270. *Untitled*. 1987.

271. *Untitled*. 1987.

272. *Untitled*. 1987.

273. *Fontana vista*. 1987.

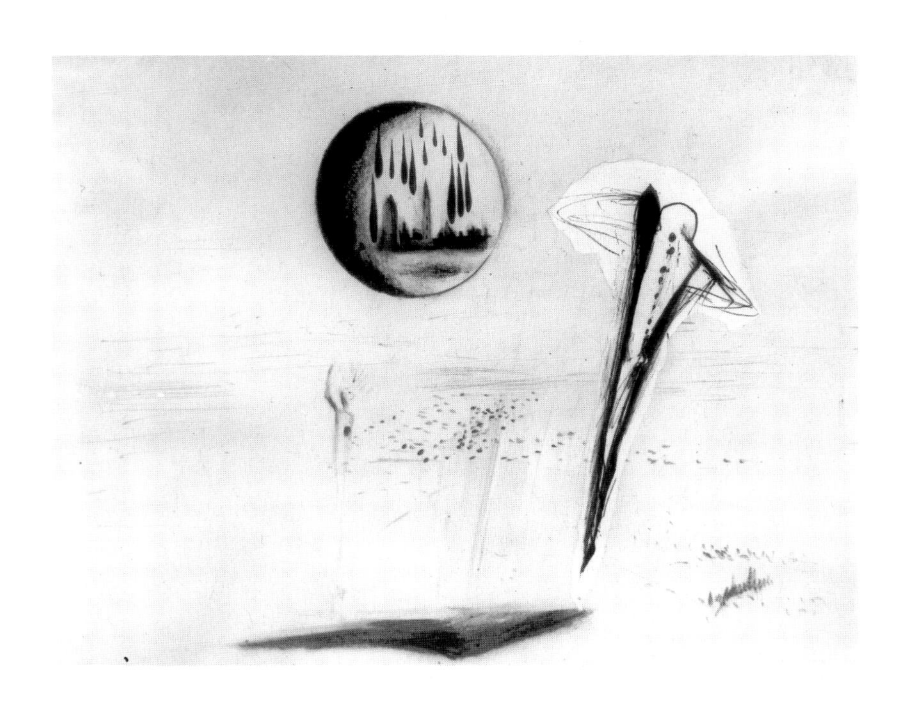

274. *Untitled*. 1987.

275. *Untitled*. 1987.

276. *Untitled*. 1987.

277. *Untitled*. 1987.

278. *Untitled*. 1987.

279. *Untitled no. 7.* 1987.

280. *Untitled*. 1987.

281. *Untitled*. 1987.

282. *Untitled no. 1.* 1987.

283. *Untitled no. 6.* 1987.

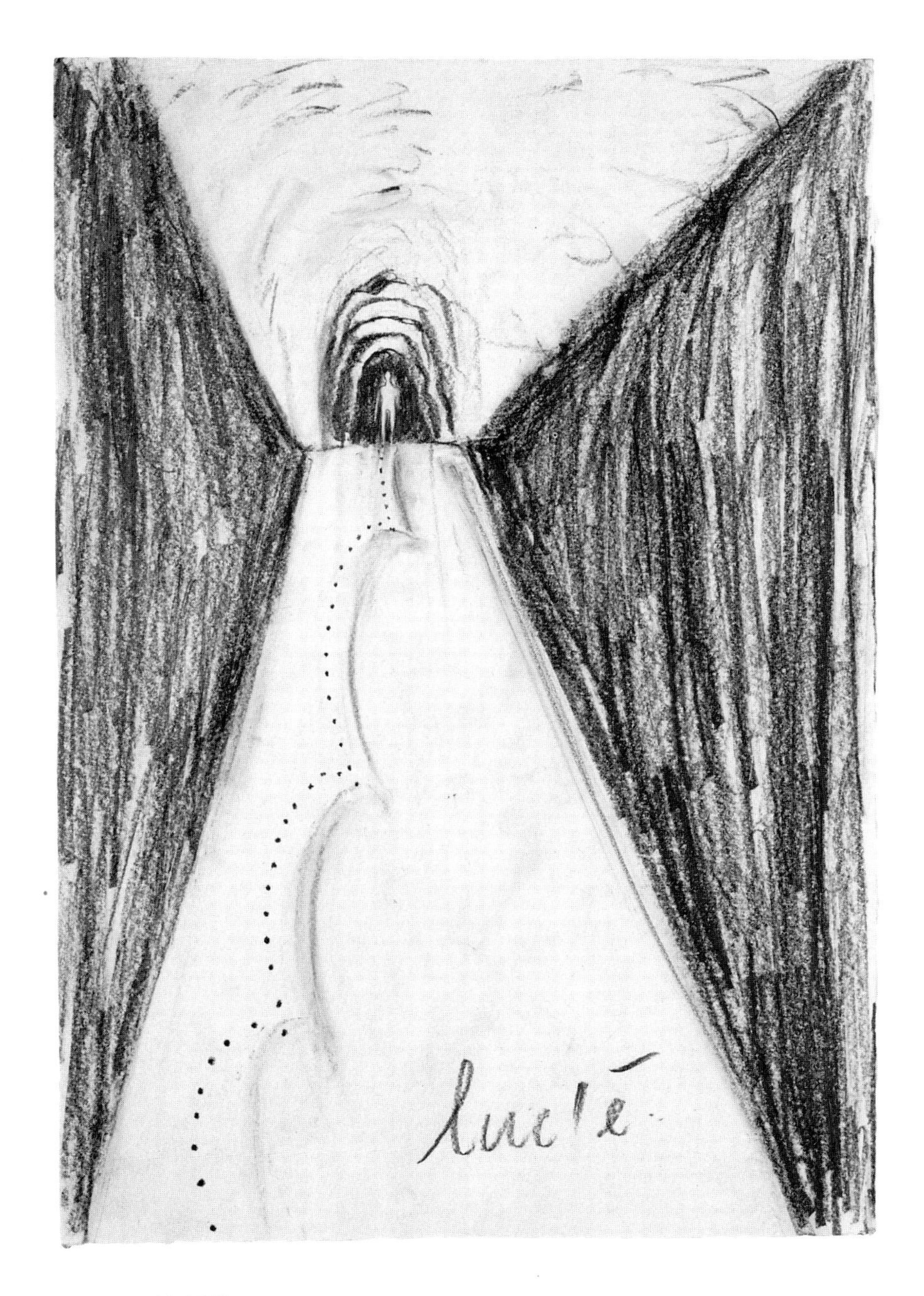

284. *Luc'é.* 1987.

1988

285. *Untitled*. 1988.

286. *Untitled*. 1988.

287. *Untitled*. 1988.

288. *Untitled*. 1988.

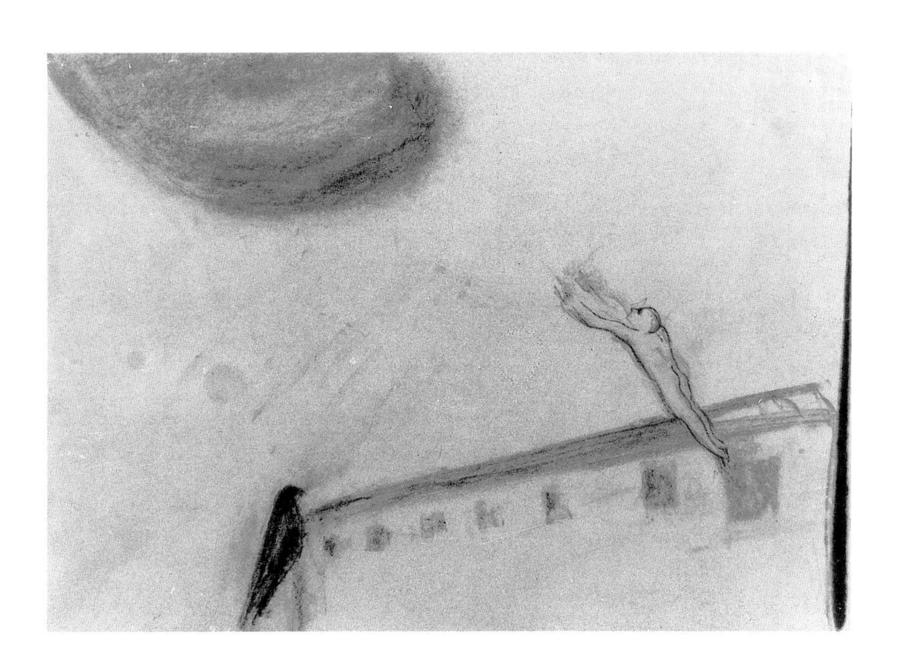

289. *Untitled*. 1988.

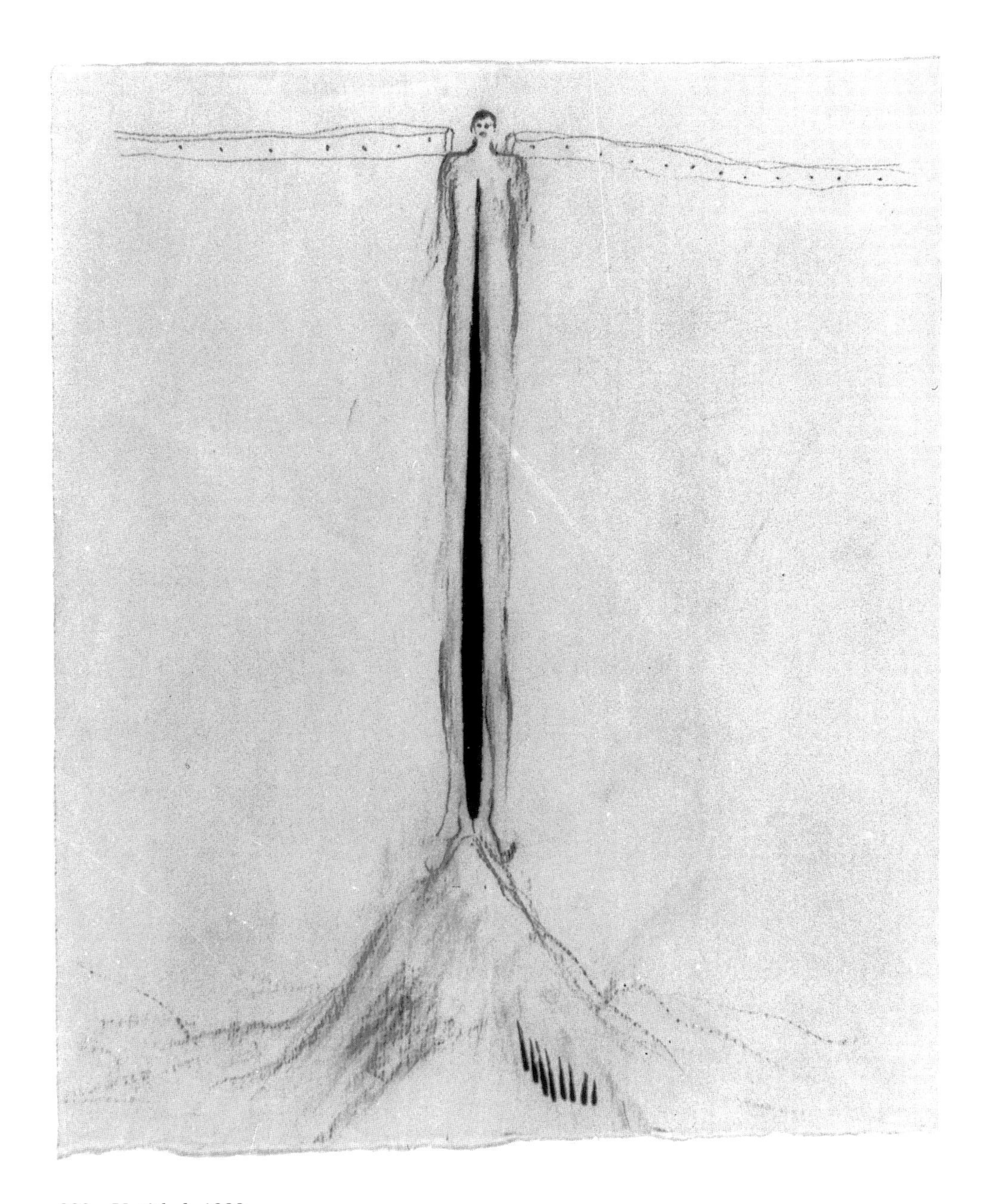

290. *Untitled*. 1988.

291. *Untitled*. 1988.

292. *Untitled*. 1988.

293. *Untitled*. 1988.

294. *Untitled*. 1988.

295. *Untitled*. 1988.

296. *Untitled*. 1988.

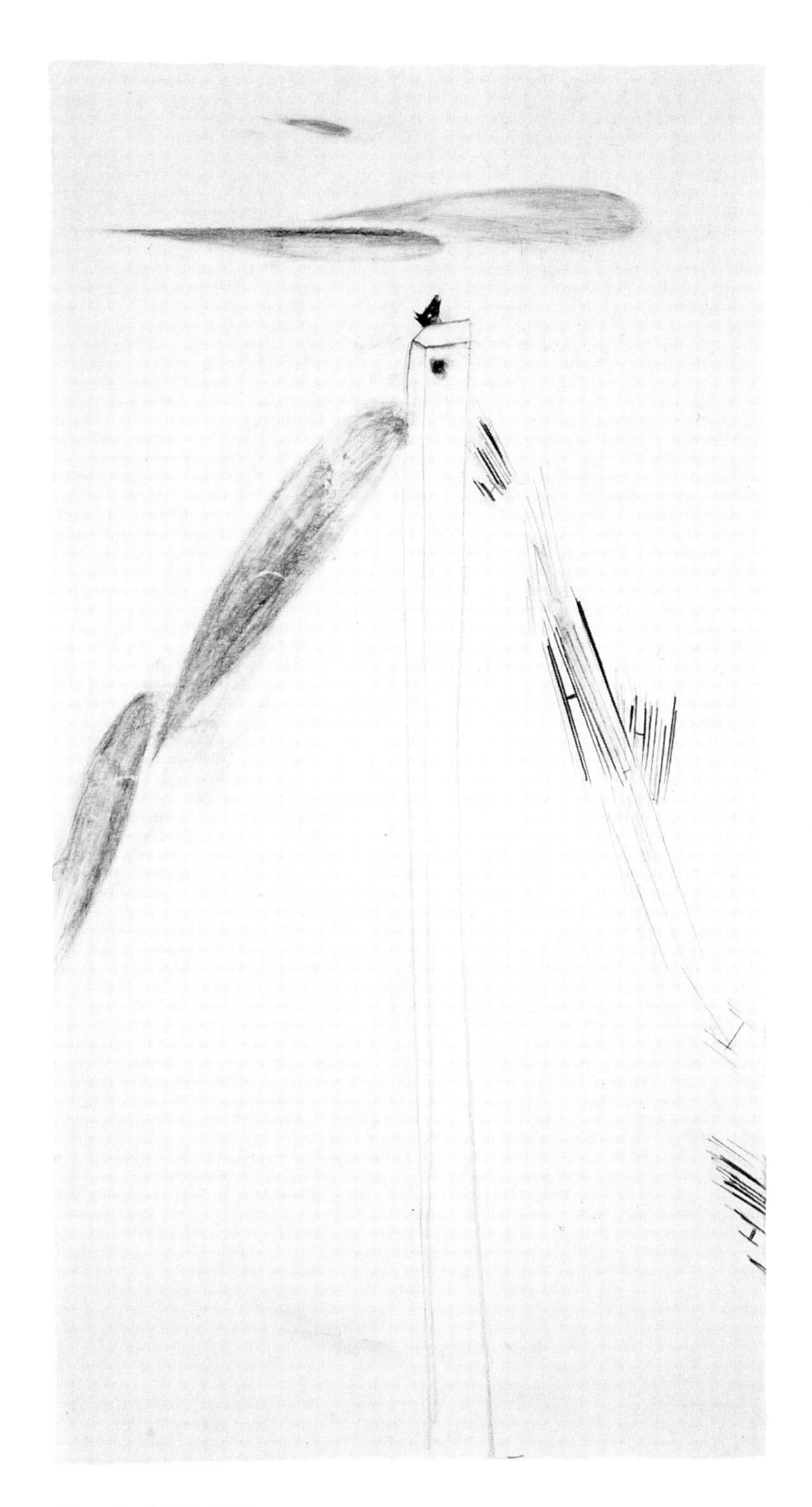

297. *Untitled*. 1988.

298. *Untitled*. 1988.

299. *Untitled*. 1988.

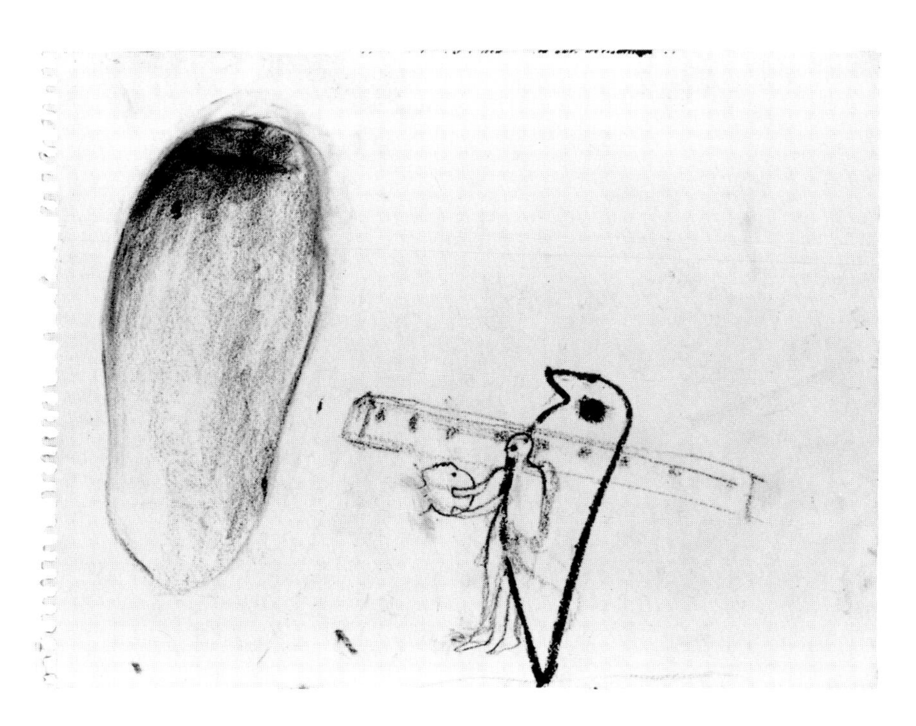

300. *Untitled*. 1988.

301. *Untitled*. 1988.

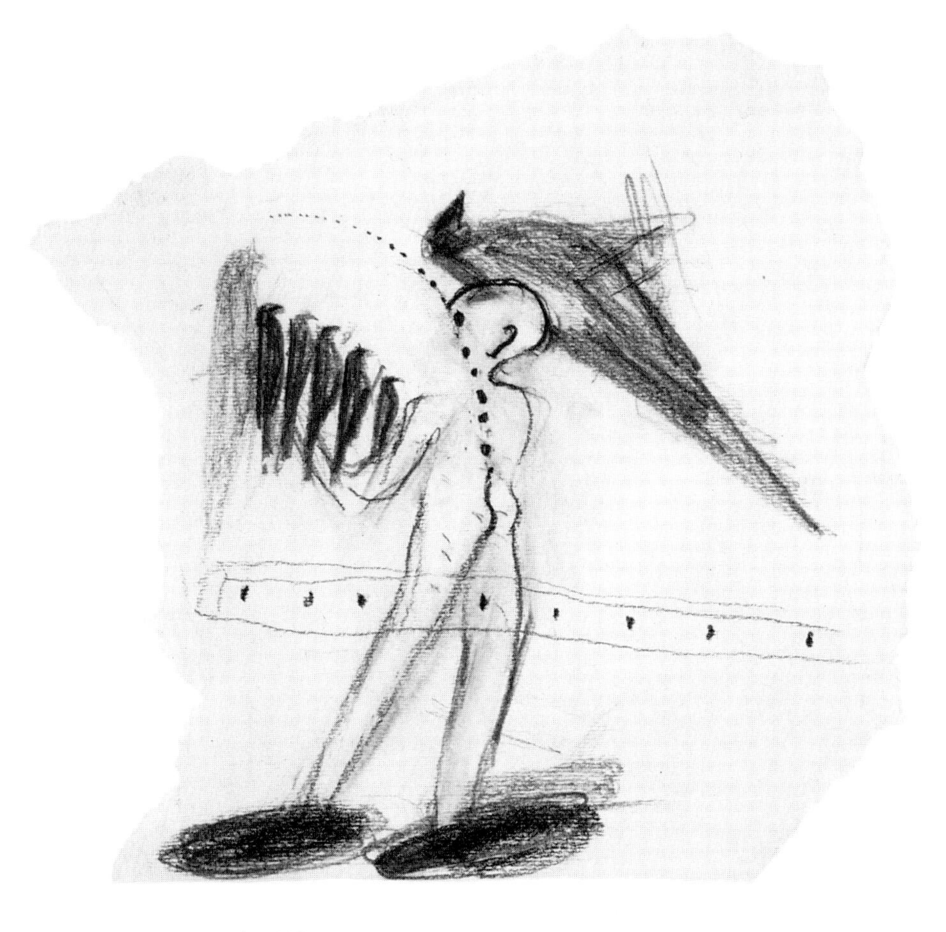

302. *Untitled*. 1988.

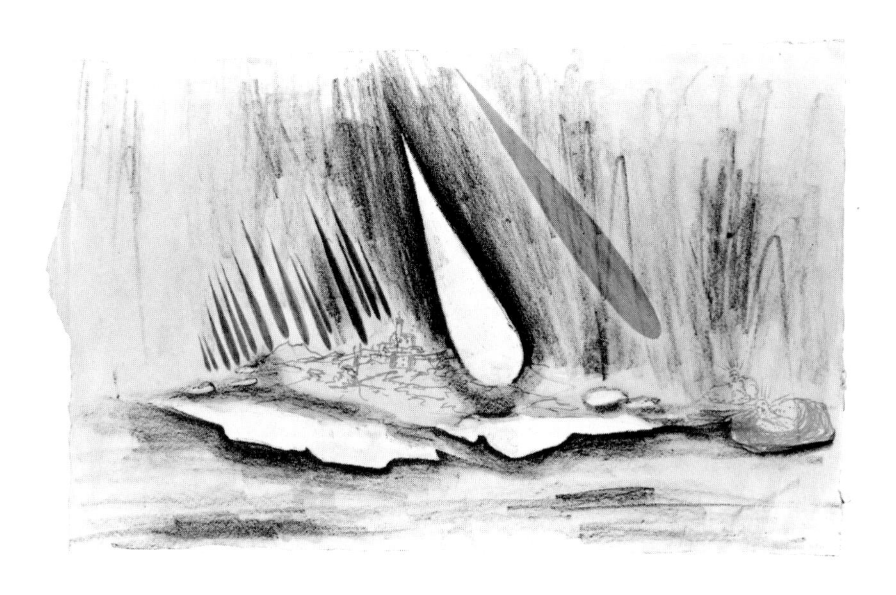

303. *Untitled*. 1988.

304. *Untitled*. 1988.

305. *Untitled*. 1988.

306. *Untitled*. 1988.

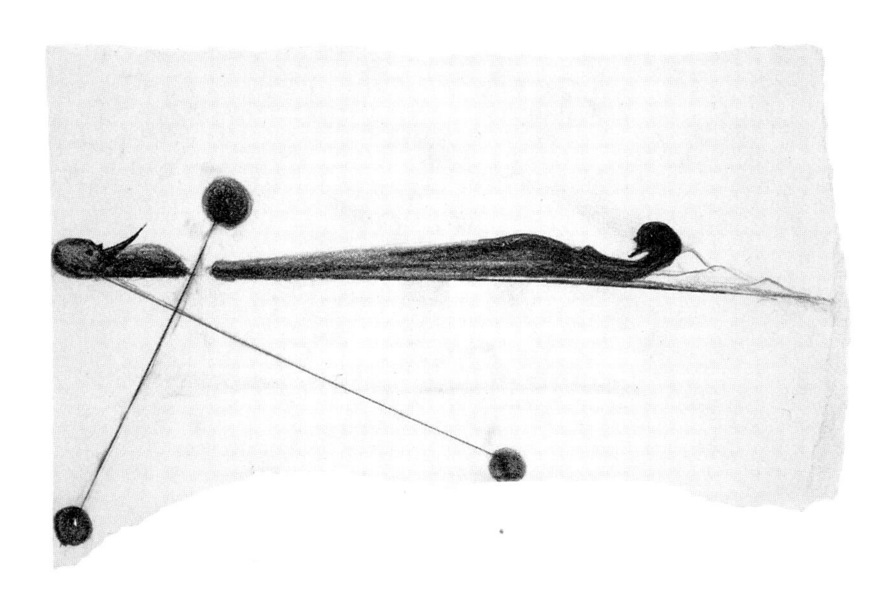

307. *Untitled*. 1988.

308. *Untitled*. 1988.

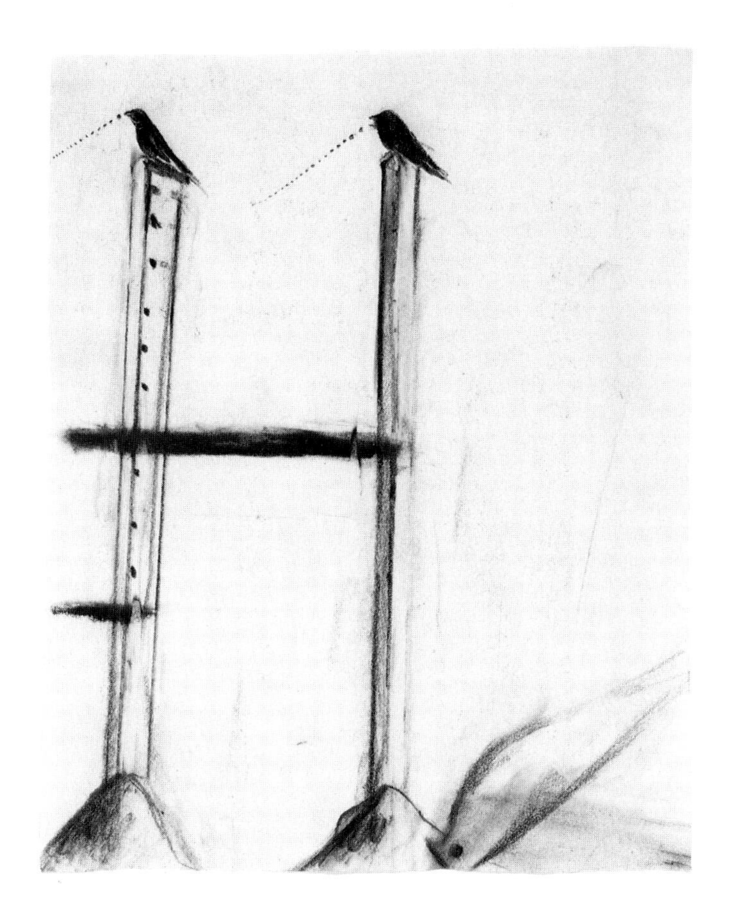

309. *Untitled*. 1988.

310. *Untitled*. 1988.

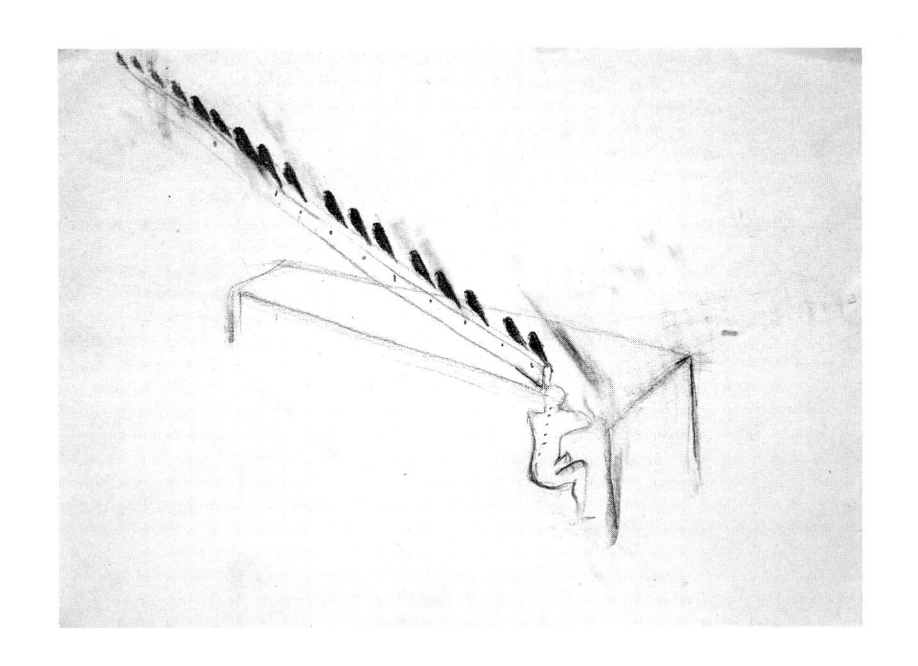

311. *Untitled*. 1988.

312. *Untitled*. 1988.

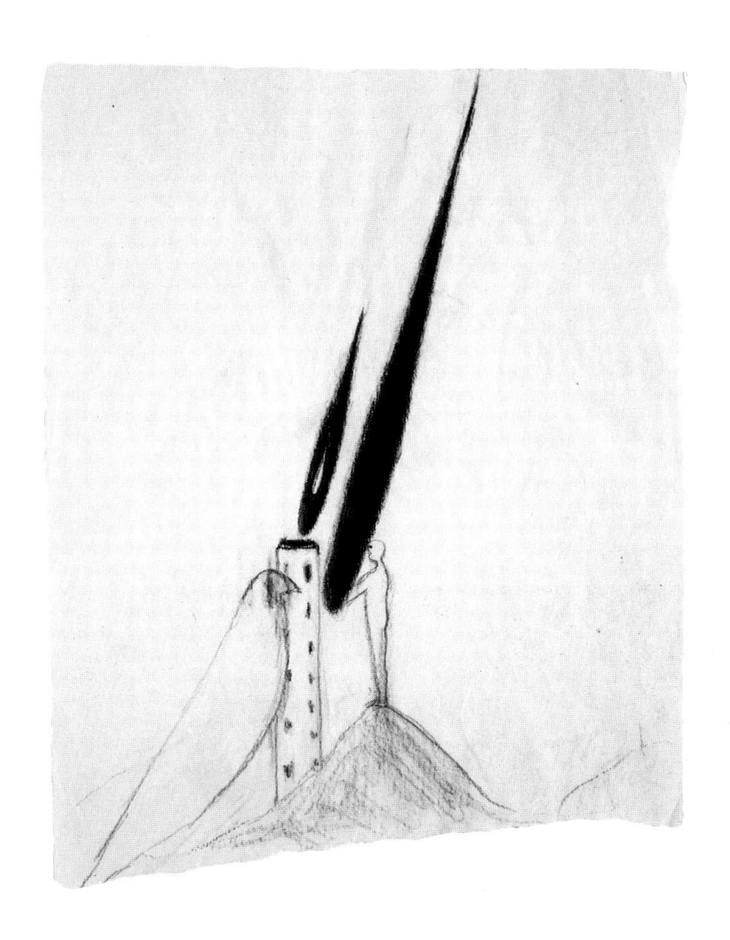

313. *Untitled*. 1988.

314. *Untitled*. 1988.

315. *Untitled*. 1988.

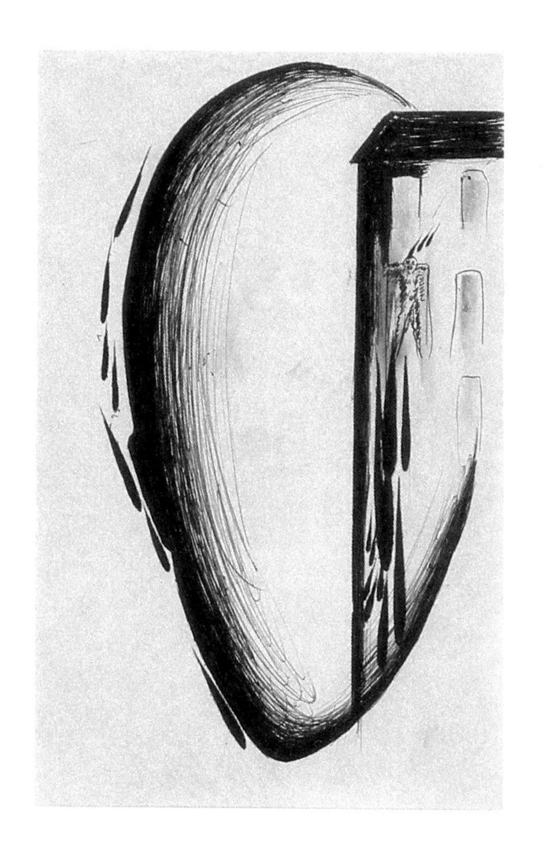

316. *Untitled.* 1988.

317. *Untitled.* 1988.

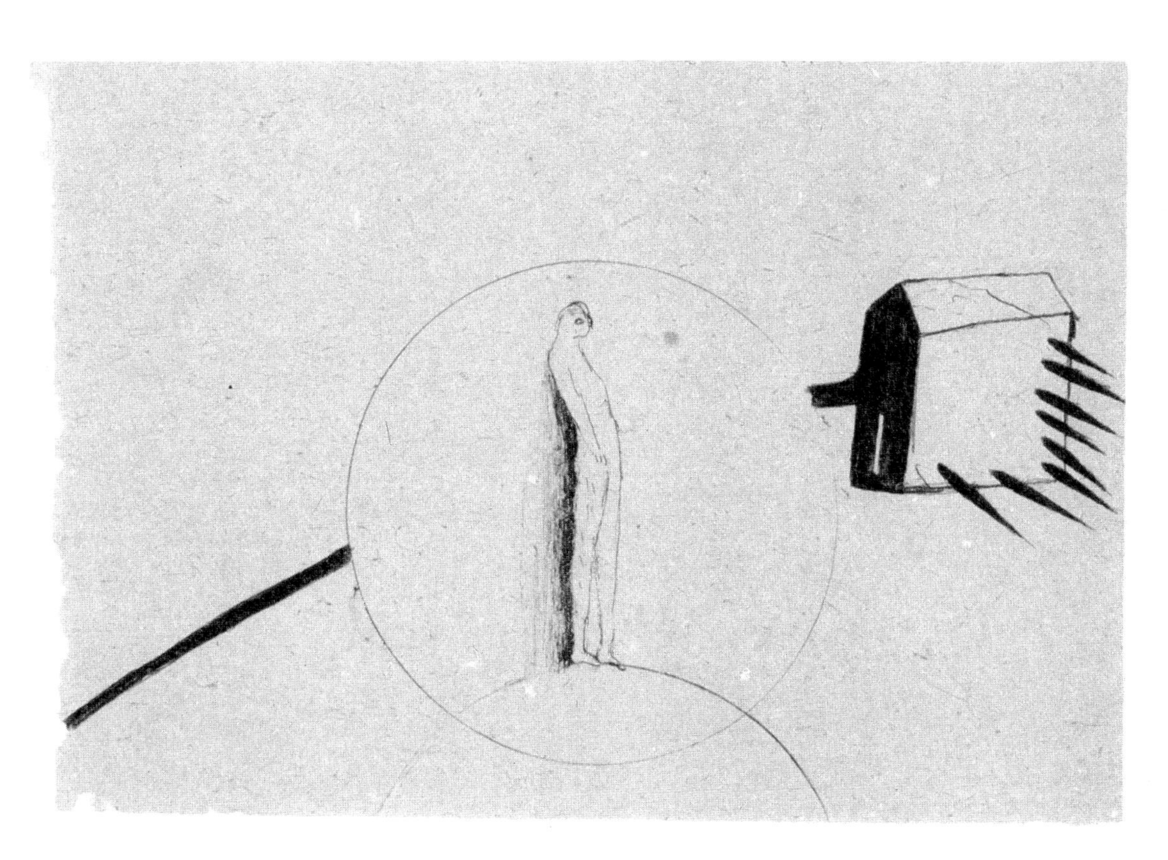

318. *Untitled*. 1988.

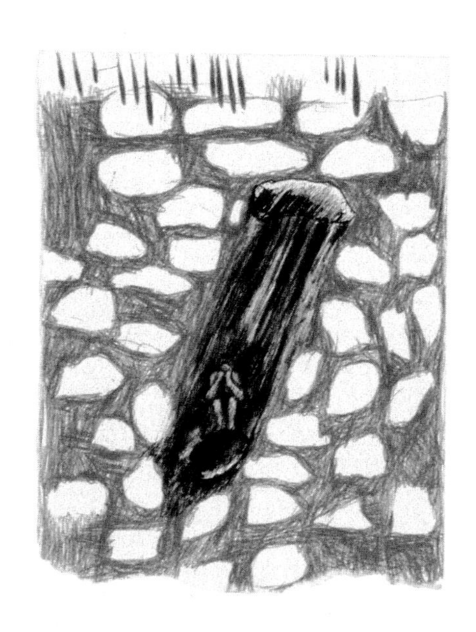

319. *Untitled.* 1988.

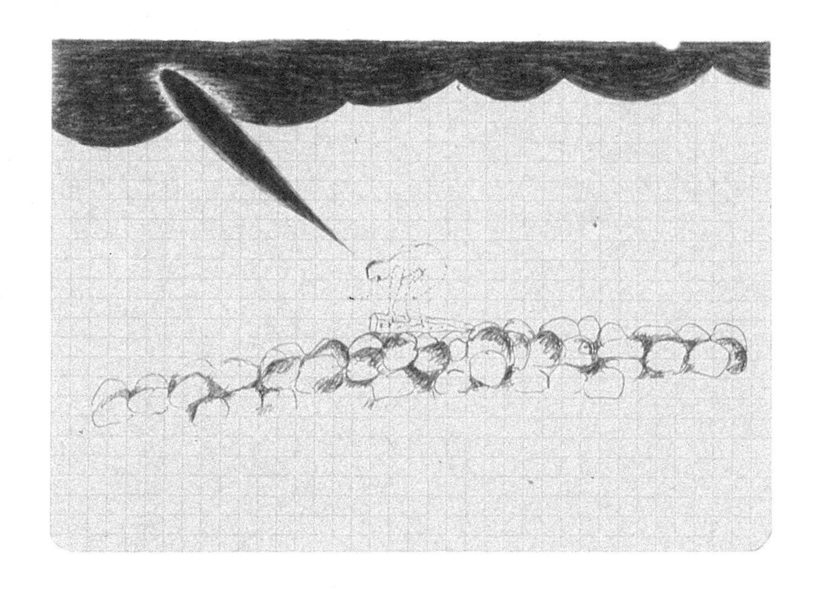

320. *Untitled.* 1988.

321. *Untitled*. 1988.

322. *Untitled*. 1988.

323. *Untitled*. 1988.

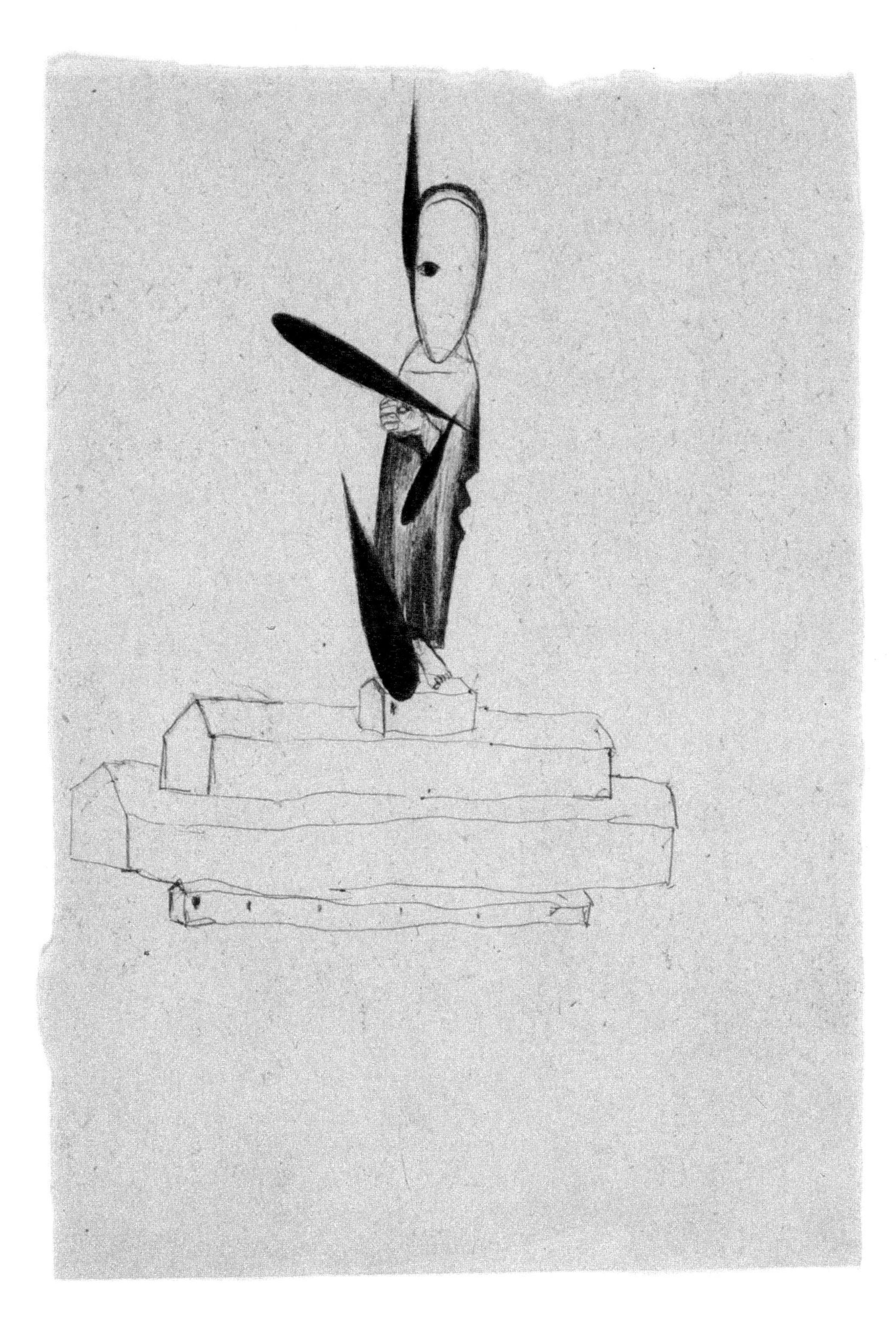

324. *Untitled*. 1988.

325. *Untitled*. 1988.

326. *Untitled*. 1988.

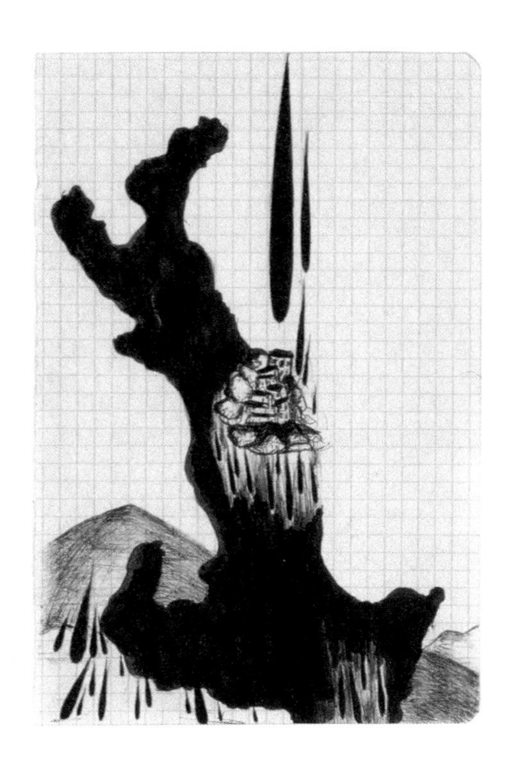

327. *Untitled.* 1988.

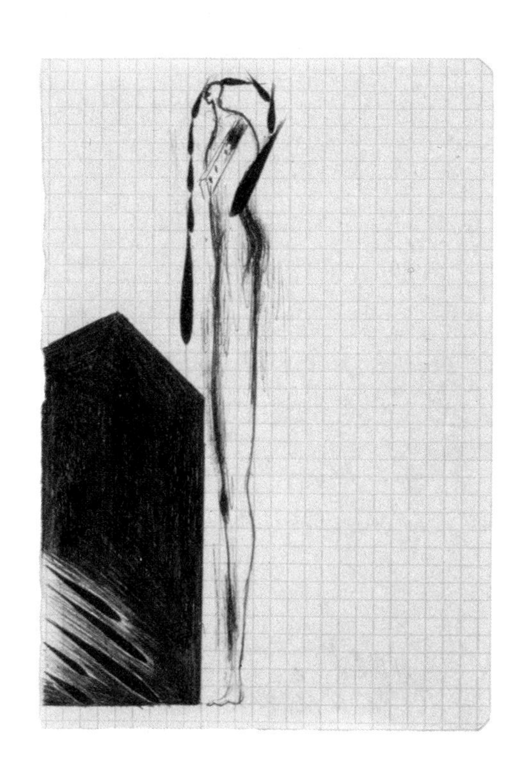

328. *Untitled.* 1988.

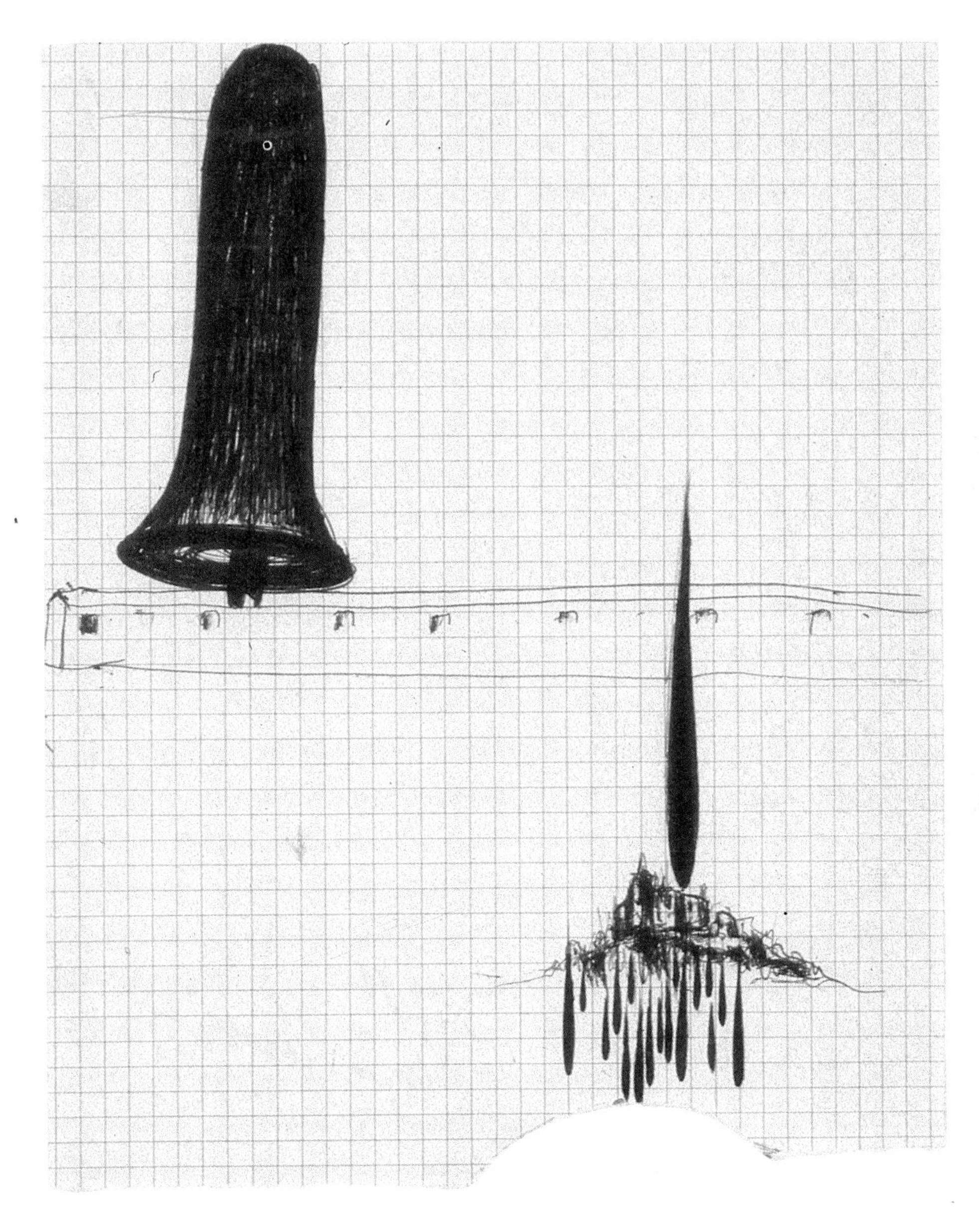

329. *Untitled*. 1988.

330. *Untitled*. 1988.

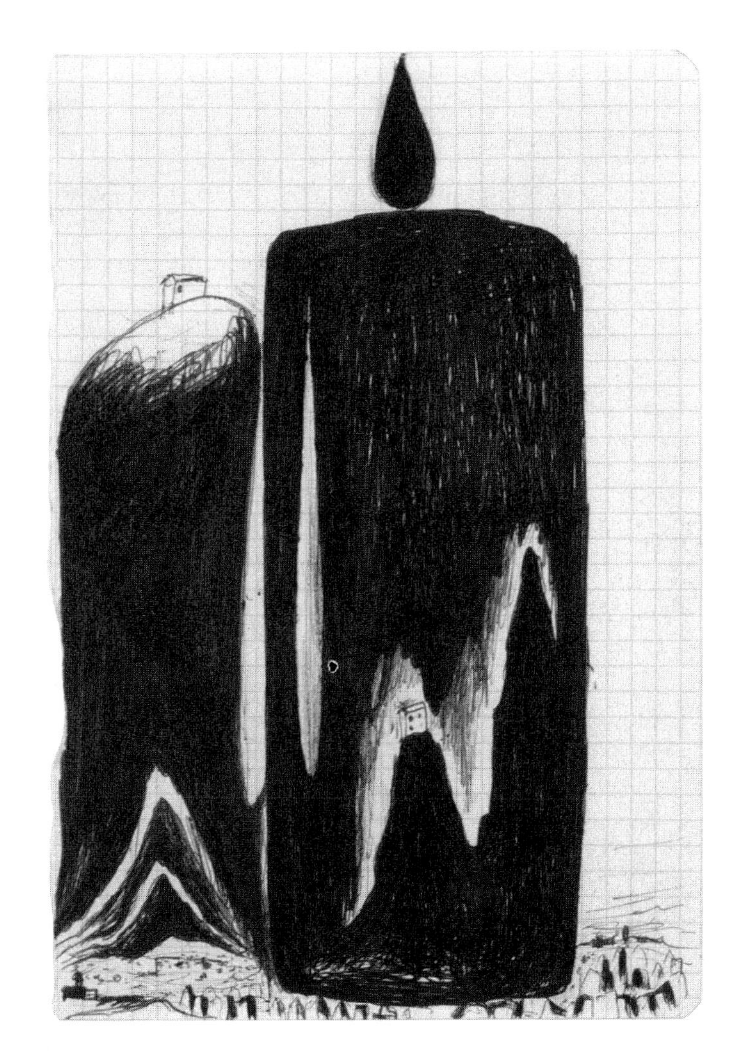

331. *Untitled.* 1988.

332. *Untitled.* 1988.

333. *Untitled.* 1988.

334. *Untitled*. 1988.

1989

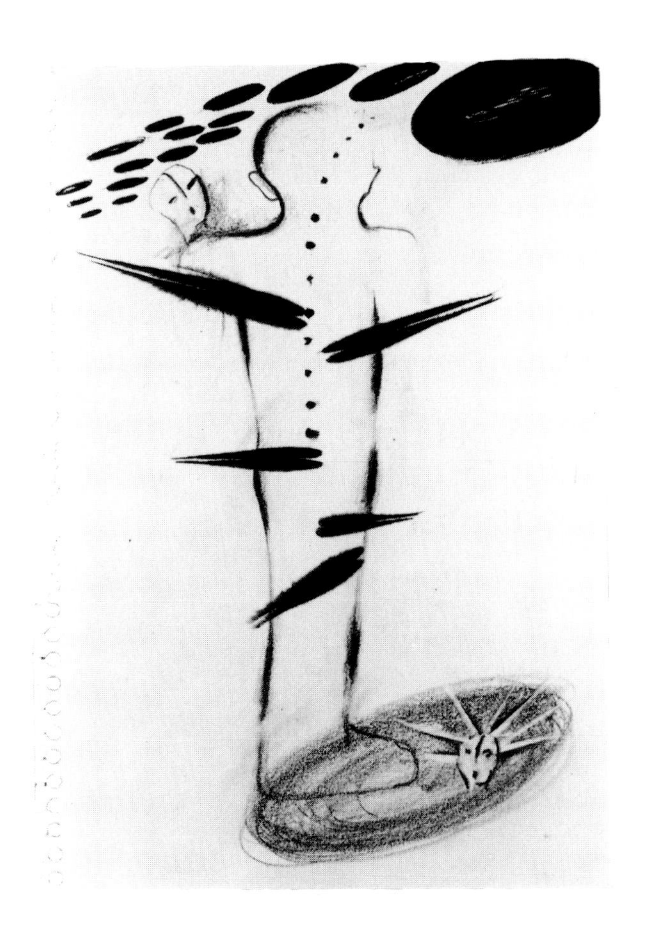

335. *Untitled, no. 5.* 1989.

336. *Untitled, no. 16.* 1989.

337. *Untitled, no. 19.* 1989.

338. *Untitled, no. 4.* 1989.

339. *Untitled, no. 2.* 1989.

340. *Untitled, no. 18.* 1989.

341. *Untitled*. 1989.

342. *Ombra vede*. 1989.

343. *Untitled.* 1989.

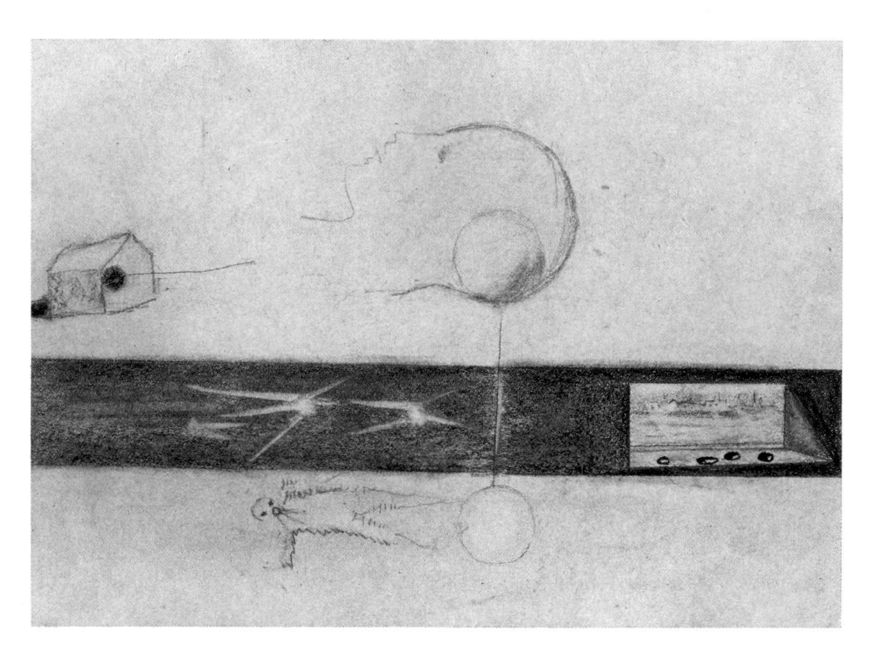

344. *Untitled.* 1989.

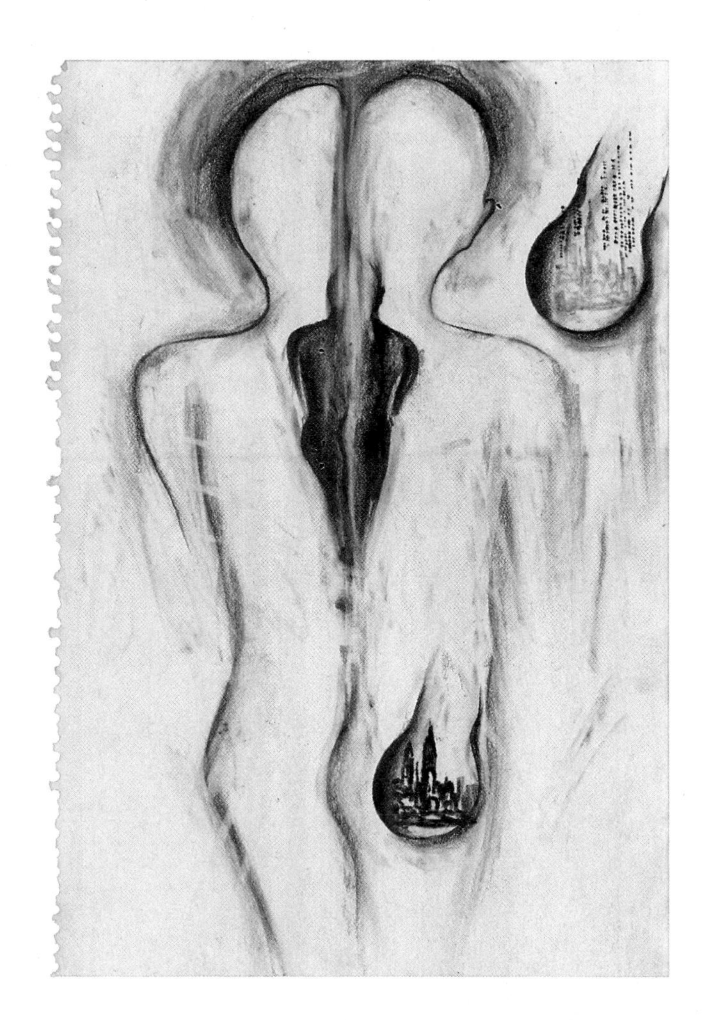

345. *Untitled.* 1989.

346. *Untitled.* 1989.

347. *Untitled.* 1989.

348. *Untitled.* 1989.

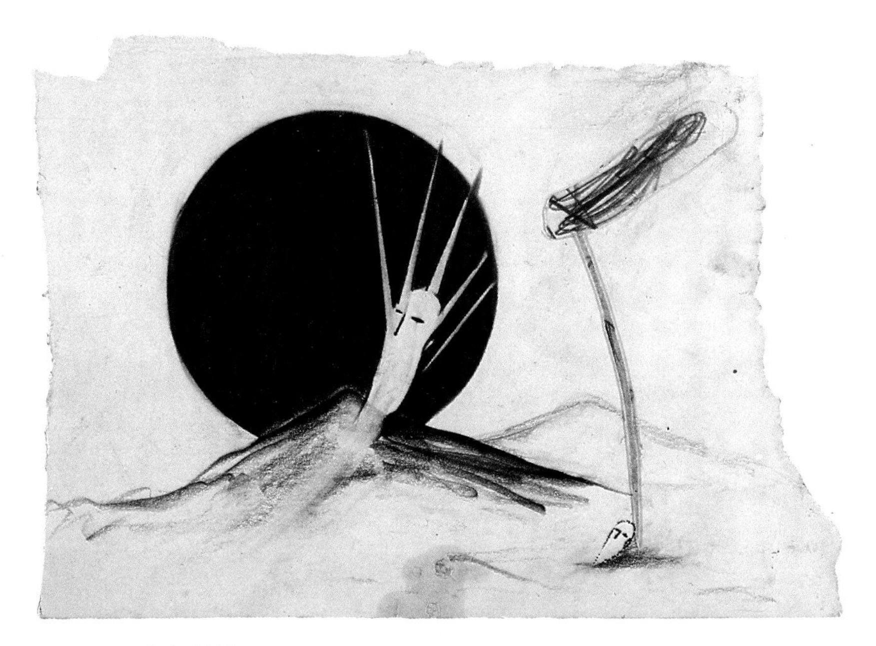

349. *Untitled*. 1989.

350. *Untitled*. 1989.

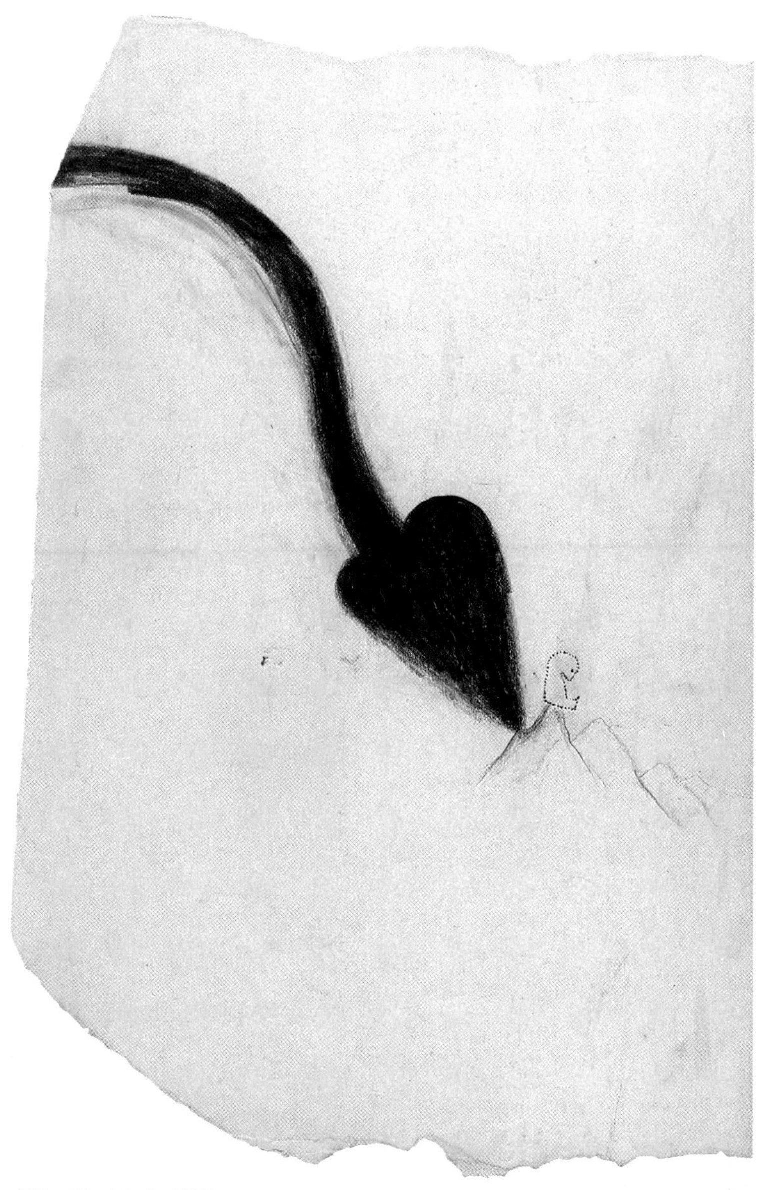

351. *Untitled*. 1989.

352. *Untitled.* 1989.

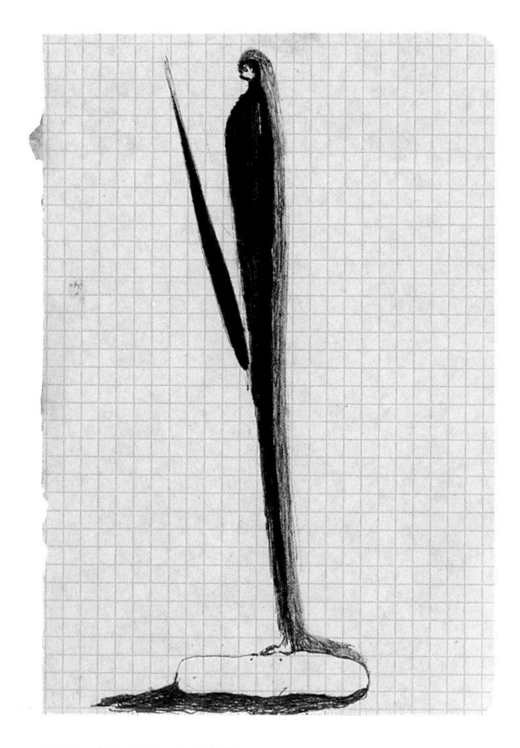

353. *Untitled.* 1989.

354. *Untitled.* 1989.

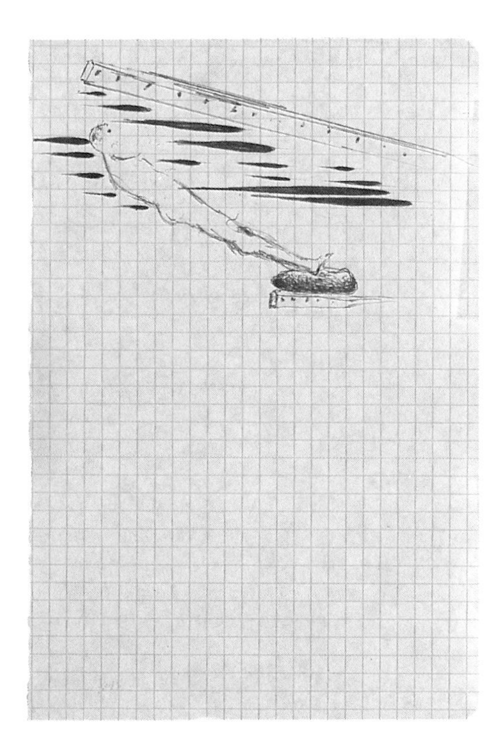

355. *Untitled.* 1989.

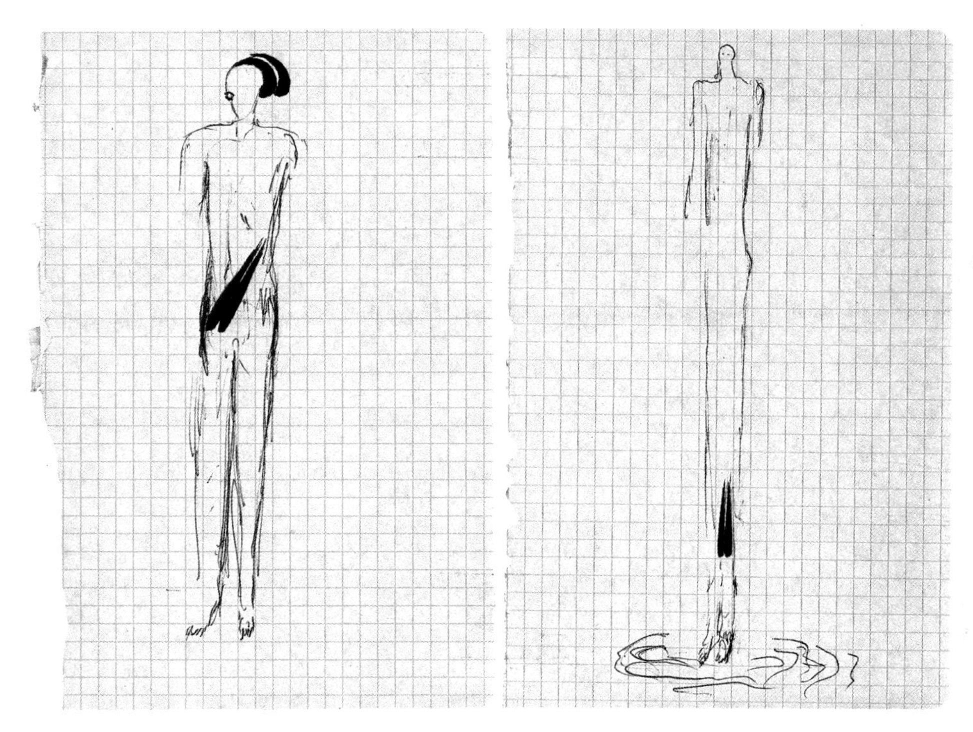

356. *Untitled.* 1989.

357. *Untitled*. 1989.

358. *Untitled*. 1989.

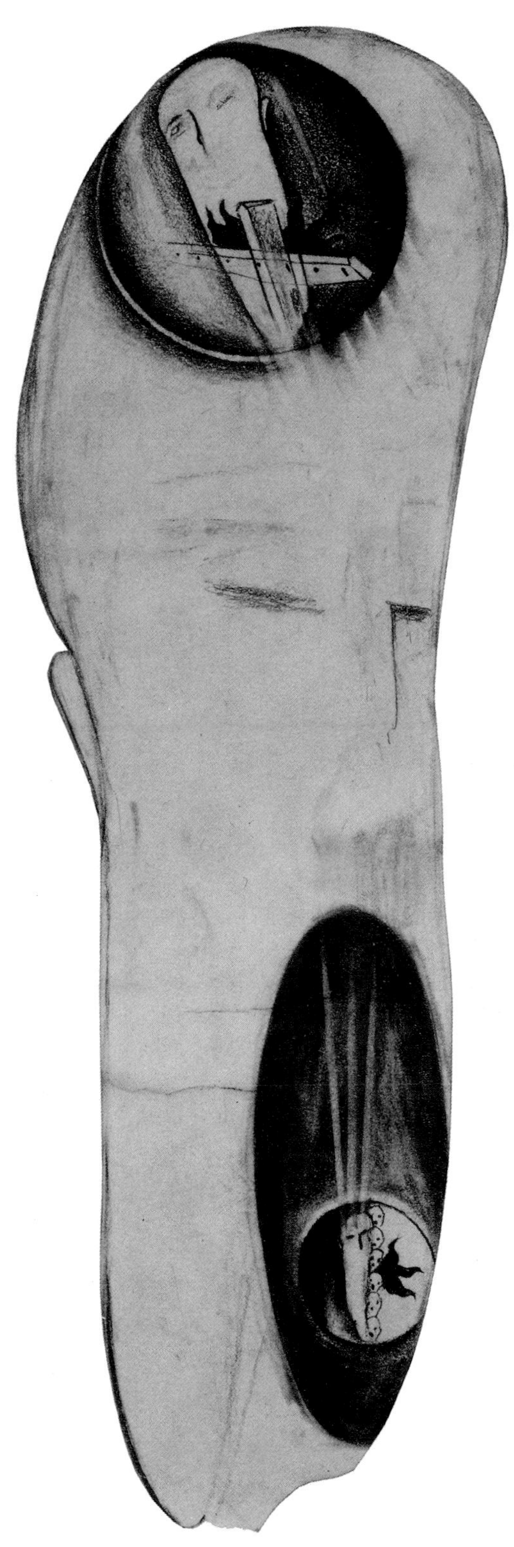

359. *Untitled*. 1989.

360. *Untitled*. 1989.

361. *Untitled.* 1989.

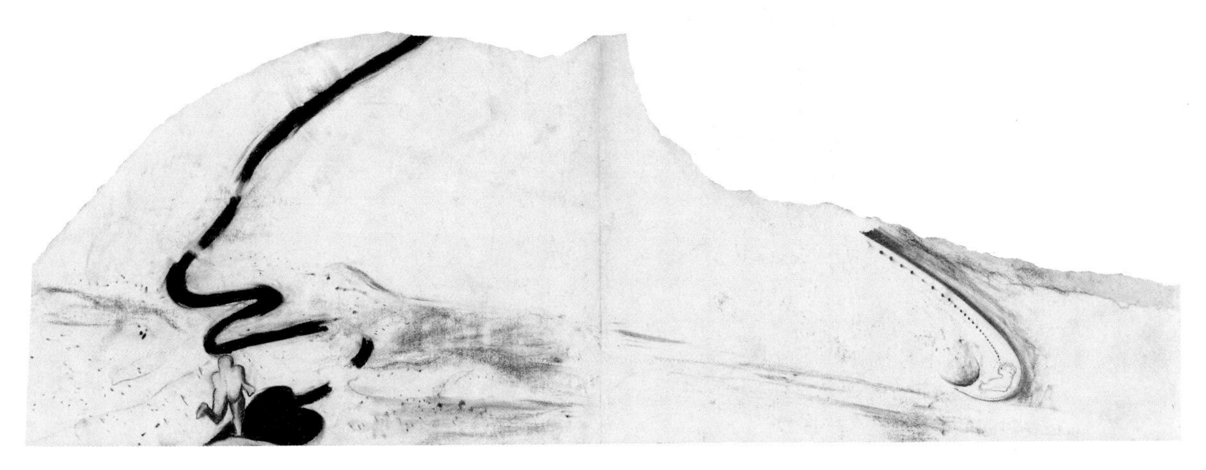

362. *Untitled.* 1989.

363. *Untitled.* 1989.

364. *Untitled.* 1989.

365. *Untitled.* 1989.

366. *Untitled*. 1989.

367. *Untitled.* 1989.

368. *Untitled.* 1989.

369. *Untitled.* 1989.

370

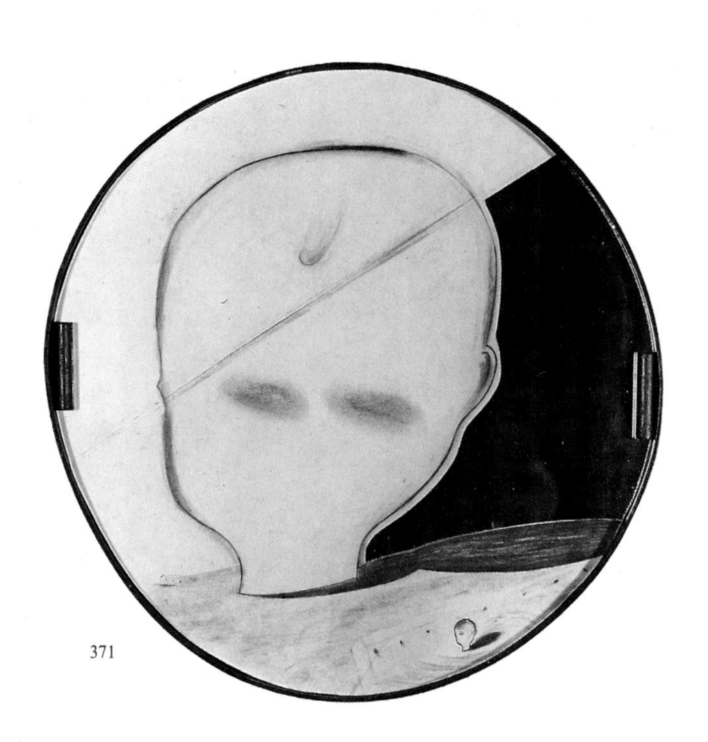

371

370 and 371. *Untitled*. 1989.

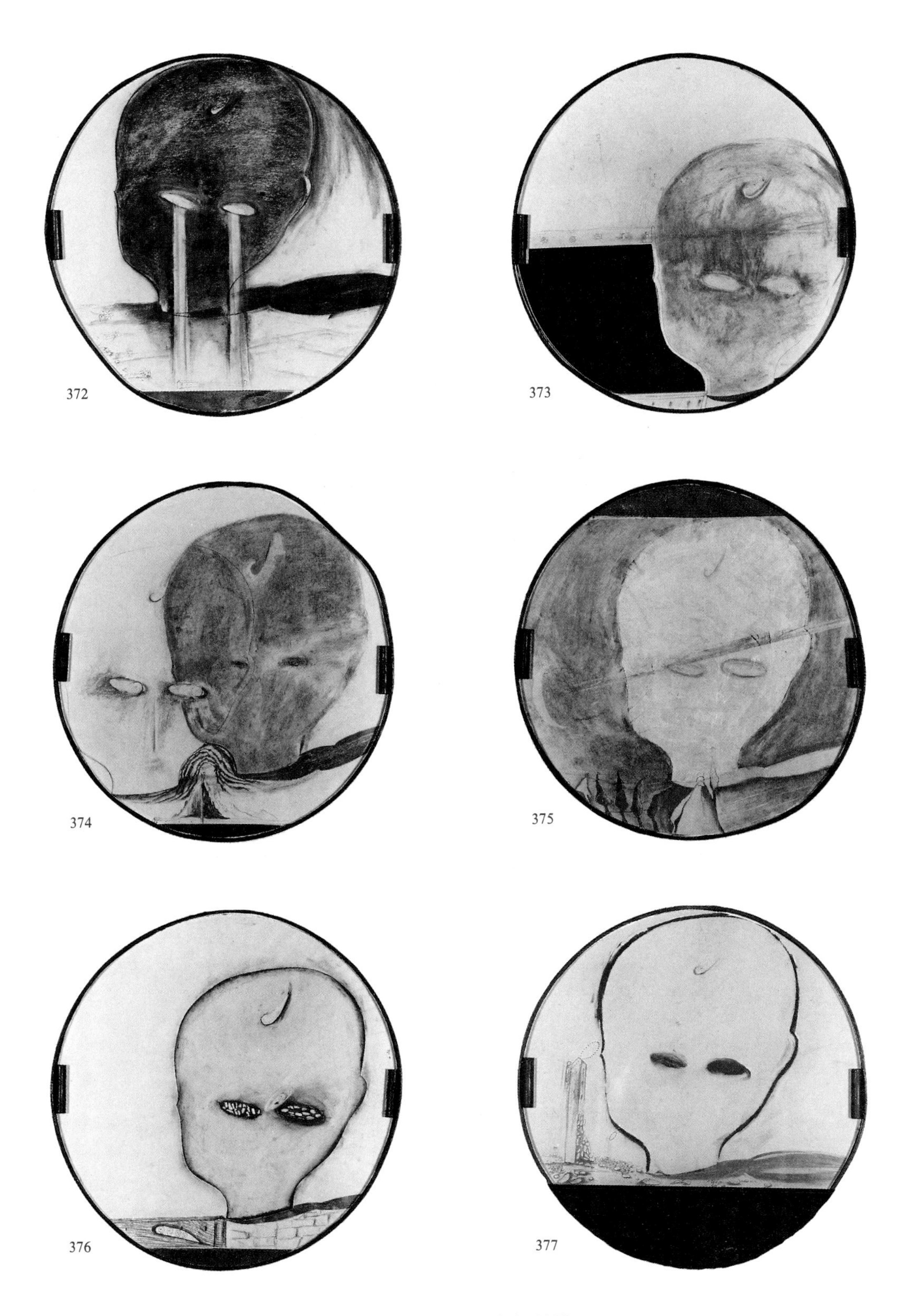

372 to 377. *Untitled*. 1989.

CATALOG

1975

1. *Untitled*. 1975.
   Watercolor, India ink and collage on silk paper,
   7¾ × 8¾ in. (19.7 × 21.3 cm).
   Private collection, Munich.

2. *Untitled*. 1975.
   Watercolor, India ink and collage on silk paper,
   7⅝ × 9¼ in. (19.4 × 23.4 cm).
   Private collection, Munich.

1976

3. *Bambino adulto*. 1976.
   (Adult Child)
   Mixed media on handmade paper,
   9½ × 13¾ in. (24 × 35 cm).
   Private collection.

4. *Untitled*. 1976.
   Mixed media on handmade paper,
   9½ × 13¾ in. (24 × 35 cm).
   Private collection.

1977

5. *Untitled*. 1977.
   Watercolor and India ink on paper,
   11¼ × 9 in. (28.6 × 23 cm).
   Groninger Museum, Groningen.

1978

6. *50 Lire, un pesce in mano*. 1978.
   (50 Lire, a Fish in the Hand)
   Pencil, charcoal, colored chalk and wash on paper,
   14⅛ × 13½ in. (36 × 34.5 cm).
   Museum Ludwig, Cologne.
   On loan from a private collection.

7. *Perché-anche-a-me*. 1978.
   (Why me too)
   Pencil, wax crayon and color on paper,
   11⅞ × 15¾ in. (30 × 40 cm).
   Private collection, Leverkusen.

8. *Immagine minore* 1978.
   (Smaller Image)
   Pencil, wax crayon, metallic paint and oil on paper,
   8⅜ × 12¼ in. (21.2 × 31 cm).
   Private collection.

9. *La cavalla azzurra*. 1978.
   (The Blue Mare)
   Pencil and wax crayon on paper,
   7 × 9½ in. (18 × 24 cm).
   Bernd Mittelsten-Schied Collection.

10. *La cavalla azzurra*. 1978.
    (The Blue Mare)
    Pencil on paper,
    7 × 9½ in. (18 × 24 cm).
    Paul Maenz Collection, Cologne.

11. *Untitled*. 1978.
    Graphite and oil on cardboard,
    11 × 15 in. (27.5 × 38 cm).
    Mario Diacono Collection, United States.

12. *Tu e voi dove andate*. 1978.
    (You and You Others, Where Are You Going)
    Pencil and gouache on paper,
    11⅞ × 15¾ in. (30 × 40 cm).
    Private collection.

13. *Vento di vino*. 1978.
    (Wind of Wine or Divine Wind)
    Wax crayon, varnish and metallic paint on paper,
    9¾ × 7 in. (24.5 × 18 cm).
    Private collection.

14. *Portami a terra in un disegno*. 1978.
    (Carry Me to Earth in a Drawing)
    Pencil, wax crayon and varnish on paper,
    11⅞ × 15⅞ in. (30 × 40.2 cm).
    Paul Maenz Collection, Cologne.

15. *Untitled.* 1978.
India ink, ballpoint and varnish
on silk paper,
18½ × 26¼ in. (47.2 × 66.5 cm).
Private collection, Munich.

16. *Untitled (Per Achille).* 1978-1979.
Oil, metallic paint and collage on paper,
11½ × 19⅜ in. (29.5 × 49.1 cm).
Private collection, Munich.

1979

17. *Vendemmia italiana.* 1979.
(Italian Grape Harvest)
India ink and blue ink on paper,
9¼ × 11⅞ in. (22.5 × 30 cm).
Elena Buchmann Collection, Basle.

18. *Untitled.* 1979.
Pencil on paper,
8⅝ × 11 in. (22 × 28 cm).
Private collection.

19. *Untitled.* 1979.
Pencil and red pencil on paper
(two superimposed sheets pasted together),
7 × 9⅝ in. (18 × 24.5 cm).
Private collection.

20. *Untitled.* 1979.
Pencil on paper,
13 × 9½ in. (33 × 24 cm).
Private collection.

21. *Immagine minore italiana.* 1979.
(Smaller Italian Image)
Pencil, wax crayon and metallic paint
on paper,
8¾ × 12¼ in. (21.2 × 31 cm).
Private collection.

22. *Untitled (Per Mercella).* 1979.
Metallic paint, red oil paint, stamp and
charcoal on silk paper,
14½ × 10⅞ in. (37 × 27.5 cm).
Private collection. Munich.

23. *E fatto di pane.* 1979.
(It's Made of Bread)
Pencil and wax crayon on paper,
13¾ × 18⅞ in. (35 × 48 cm).
Groninger Museum, Groningen.

24. *Mare adriatico pesco.* 1979.
(I Fish the Adriatic Sea)
Pencil and charcoal on paper,
15⅝ × 11⅞ in. (39.8 × 30 cm).
Peter Blum Collection, New York.

25. *Disegni marchigiani.* 1979.
(Drawings of The Marches)
Pencil and wax crayon on paper,
11⅞ × 15¾ in. (30 × 40 cm).
Galerie Paul Maenz, Cologne.

26. *Untitled.* 1979.
Pencil on paper,
12⅞ × 17¼ in. (32.5 × 44 cm).
Galerie Bruno Bischofberger, Zurich.

27. *Non lo posso dire.* 1979.
(I Cannot Say It)
Pencil and watercolor on paper,
11⅝ × 15¾ in. (29.8 × 40 cm).
Private collection, Munich.

28. *Campagna animalosa.* 1979.
(Field of Animals)
Pencil and tempera on paper,
11⅞ × 15¾ in. (30 × 40 cm).
Private collection, Basle.

29. *Tutti i disegni della'Italia centrale.* 1979.
(All the Drawings of Central Italy)
Pencil and wax crayon on paper,
11⅝ × 15⅞ in. (29.9 × 40.1 cm).
Kupferstichkabinett,
Öffentliche Kunstsammlung, Basle.

30. *Disegno al buio sul mare.* 1979.
(Sea Drawing in the Dark)
Pencil, wax crayon, ballpoint and varnish
on paper,
11⅞ × 15¾ in. (30 × 40 cm).
Private collection, Munich.

31. *Adriatico! Mare disegnato per me*. 1979.
(The Adriatic! A Sea Designed by Me)
Pencil and charcoal on paper,
11 6/8 × 15¾ in. (29.9 × 40 cm).
Kupferstichkabinett,
Öffentliche Kunstsammlung, Basle.

32. *Untitled*. 1979.
Pencil and wax crayon on paper,
13 6/8 × 19 in. (34.7 × 48.5 cm).
Galerie Paul Maenz, Cologne.

33. *La scopa dell'amore*. 1979.
(The Sweeping Brush of Love)
Pencil and black and colored chalk
on paper,
11⅞ × 15¾ in. (30 × 40 cm).
Kunsthaus Zürich, Graphische Sammlung,
Zurich.

34. *Ecclissi del sole*. 1979.
(Eclipse of the Sun)
Charcoal and ballpoint on paper,
15½ × 11½ in. (39.5 × 29.5 cm).
Galerie Bruno Bischofberger, Zurich.

35. *Uomo del temporale*. 1979.
(Man of the Storm)
Retouched in 1981-1982.
Charcoal, pencil and red ink on paper,
15⅜ × 11⅝ in. (39.8 × 30 cm).
Private collection, Basle.

1980

36. *L'angelo*. 1980.
(The Angel)
Charcoal, pencil and ink on paper,
15½ × 11¾ in. (39.5 × 29.9 cm).
Galerie Bruno Bischofberger, Zurich.

37. *La casa*. 1980.
(The House)
Pencil on paper,
15¾ × 8¼ in. (39 × 21 cm).
Z. Mis Collection, Brussels.

38. *Santo albero*. 1980.
(Sacred Tree)
Charcoal on paper,
13¾ × 17½ in. (34.9 × 44.5 cm).
Private collection, United States.

39. *Palla-santa*. 1980.
(Holy Sphere)
Pencil and fixative on paper,
17¼ × 12½ in. (44 × 31.9 cm).
The Museum of Modern Art, New York.
Contemporary European Drawing Fund.

40. *Disegno minore marchigiano*. 1980.
(Smaller Drawing of The Marches)
Pencil on paper,
18¾ × 13⅜ in. (47.5 × 34 cm).
Private collection, Basle.

41. *Untitled*. 1980.
Charcoal and tempera on paper,
12¾ × 17½ in. (32.5 × 44.5 cm).
Peter Blum Collection, New York.

42. *Pesci santi da Ancona*. 1980.
(Holy Fish of Ancona)
Pencil and charcoal on paper,
11 6/8 × 15¾ in. (29.9 × 40 cm).
Kupferstichkabinett,
Öffentliche Kunstsammlung, Basle.

43. *Al buio sul mare adriatico*. 1980.
(In the Dark on the Adriatic Sea)
Preliminary sketch for the
"Immagine Feroce" (Fierce Image)
portfolio, 1981, sheet no. 1.
Charcoal on paper,
14⅜ × 19½ in. (36.5 × 49.5 cm).
Peter Blum Collection, New York.

44. *Tutte le montagne sono sante*. 1980.
(All Mountains are Holy)
"Immagine Feroce," 1981, sheet no. 3.
Charcoal on paper,
17⅜ × 12 6/8 in. (44.2 × 32.5 cm).
Peter Blum Collection, New York.

45. *Immagine minore marchigiana*. 1980.
(Smaller Image of The Marches)
Preparatory sketch for the
"Immagine Feroce" portfolio,
1981, sheet no. 2.
Charcoal and pencil on paper,
12⅜ × 17¼ in. (31.6 × 44 cm).
Peter Blum Collection, New York.

46. *Il santo di Loreto*. 1980.
(The Saint of Loreto)
Preparatory sketch for the
"Immagine Feroce" portfolio,
1981, sheet no. 4.
Charcoal on paper,
17¼ × 12⅝ in. (44 × 32 cm).
Peter Blum Collection, New York.

47. *Tutti i pesci devono andare piano*. 1980.
(All Fish Should Walk Slowly)
Preparatory sketch for the
"Immagine Feroce" portfolio,
1981, sheet no. 5.
Charcoal and India ink on paper,
13¾ × 19⅝ in. (35 × 50 cm).
Peter Blum Collection, New York.

48. *Disegno feroce di 1980*. 1980.
(Fierce Design from 1980)
Pencil, India ink and chalk on paper,
19½ × 15 in. (49.7 × 38 cm).
Solomon R. Guggenheim Museum,
New York.
Norman Dubrov Donation, 1985.

49. *Untitled*. 1980.
(Portrait of Francesco Clemente)
Charcoal on cardboard,
37¼ × 8¾ in. (94.4 × 22.1 cm).
Private collection, Munich.

50. *5 monti sono santi*. 1980.
(5 Mountains Are Holy)
Wax crayon and ballpoint on paper,
8⅝ × 12¼ in. (22 × 31 cm).
Paul Maenz Collection, Cologne.

1981

51. *Fontana innamorata*. 1981.
(Enamoured Fountain)
Charcoal, ink and India ink wash on paper,
11⅞ × 8⅞ in. (30 × 22.5 cm).
Kunsthaus Zürich, Graphische Sammlung,
Zurich.

52. *Preghiera del'arbero*. 1981.
(The Tree's Prayer)
Pencil and charcoal on paper,
15¾ × 5⅞ in. (40 × 15 cm).
Courtesy of the Galerie Paul Maenz,
Cologne.

53. *Casa terrestre*. 1981.
(Terrestrial House)
Charcoal on paper,
15¾ × 11⅞ in. (40 × 30 cm).
Private collection, Leverkusen.

54. *Miracolo di legno*. 1981.
(Miracle of Wood)
Wax crayon and pencil on paper,
19½ × 17¼ in. (49.6 × 44 cm).
Paul Maenz Collection, Cologne.

55. *Il santo delle tempeste*. 1981.
(The Saint of the Tempests)
Pencil, charcoal and marking pen on paper,
11¾ × 15¾ in. (29.9 × 40 cm).
Kupferstichkabinett,
Öffentliche Sammlung, Basle.

56. *Trasporto angelico*. 1981.
(Angelic Transport)
Pencil, charcoal and ballpoint on paper,
11⅞ × 15½ in. (30 × 39.5 cm).
Lilott and Erik Berganus Collection,
Hamburg.

57. *Santo, santo*. 1981.
(Saint, Saint)
Pencil and charcoal on paper,
15¾ × 11¾ in. (40 × 29.8 cm).
Kupferstichkabinett,
Öffentliche Kunstsammlung, Basle.

58. *Untitled.* 1981.
Charcoal on paper,
19¼ × 14 in. (49 × 35.5 cm).
Courtesy of Thomas Ammann, Zurich.

59. *Untitled.* 1981.
Charcoal on paper,
13½ × 19¼ in. (34.5 × 49 cm).
Courtesy of Thomas Ammann, Zurich.

60. *Untitled.* 1981.
Charcoal on paper,
11⅜ × 17 in. (29 × 43 cm).
Courtesy of Thomas Ammann, Zurich.

61. *Untitled.* 1981.
Charcoal on paper,
13½ × 19½ in. (34.5 × 49.5 cm).
Courtesy of Thomas Ammann, Zurich.

62. *Untitled.* 1981.
Charcoal on paper,
12⅜ × 17¾ in. (31.5 × 45 cm).
Courtesy of Thomas Ammann, Zurich.

63. *Untitled.* 1981.
Charcoal on paper,
18⅞ × 27½ in. (48 × 70 cm).
Courtesy of Thomas Ammann, Zurich.

64. *Untitled.* 1981.
Charcoal on paper,
24¾ × 9⅞ in. (62.5 × 25 cm).
Courtesy of Thomas Ammann, Zurich.

65. *Untitled.* 1981
Charcoal on paper,
13½ × 13¾ in. (49.5 × 35 cm).
Courtesy of Thomas Ammann, Zurich.

66. *Il vento delle pietre.* 1981.
(The Wind of Stones)
Charcoal and pencil on paper,
15½ × 11⅞ in. (39.5 × 30 cm).
Peter Blum Collection, New York.

67. *I fiori de pietra.* 1981.
(The Flowers of Stone)
Charcoal and green ballpoint on paper,
11¾ × 15½ in. (29.8 × 39.5 cm).
Peter Blum Collection, New York.

68. *Untitled.* 1981.
Charcoal, pencil and green pen on paper,
14½ × 18½ in. (36.8 × 47 cm).
Private collection, United States.

69. *Miracolo.* 1981.
(Miracle)
Charcoal and pencil on paper,
15½ × 11⅞ in. (39.5 × 30 cm).
Courtesy of the Galerie Paul Maenz, Cologne.

70. *La pietra del tempo.* 1981.
(The Stone of Time)
Charcoal on paper,
13¾ × 11 in. (35 × 28 cm).
Galerie Paul Maenz, Cologne.

71. *Il miracolo delle montagne.* 1981.
(The Miracle of the Mountains)
Charcoal and tempera on paper,
15¾ × 11⅞ in. (40 × 30 cm).
Private collection.

72. *Il miracolo delle montagne.* 1981.
(The Miracle of the Mountains)
Charcoal and red ink on paper,
15¾ × 11⅞ in. (40 × 30 cm).
Private collection, Basle.

73. *Le case vanno in discesa.* 1981.
(The Houses Go Downhill)
Pencil and oil on paper,
12 × 9¼ in. (30.5 × 23.5 cm).
Private collection.

74. *Pane santo.* 1981.
(Holy Bread)
Charcoal on paper,
15½ × 11⅝ in. (39.5 × 29.7 cm).
Peter Blum Collection, New York.

75. *I peccati dei sassi.* 1981.
(The Sins of the Stones)
Pencil, charcoal and ink on paper,
17 × 12⅞ in. (43 × 32.7 cm).
Galerie Bruno Bischofberger, Zurich.

76. *Untitled.* Around 1981.
Pencil, pastel and green marking pen on paper,
11⅞ × 15¾ in. (30 × 40 cm).
Hamburger Kunsthalle, Hamburg.

77. *Il sentimento di un eroe.* 1981.
(The Feeling of a Hero)
Charcoal, pencil and wax crayon on paper,
11⅝ × 15¾ in. (29.8 × 40 cm).
Galerie Bruno Bischofberger, Zurich.

78. *Per la mia fede.* 1981.
(For My Faith)
Charcoal and pencil on paper,
11⅝ × 15¾ in. (29.7 × 40 cm).
Galerie Bruno Bischofberger, Zurich.

79. *Untitled.* 1981.
Charcoal, pencil and green ballpoint on paper,
11⅞ × 15¾ in. (30 × 40 cm).
Galerie Bruno Bischofberger, Zurich.

1982

80. *Tesoro misterioso.* 1982
(Mysterious Treasure)
Charcoal and India ink on paper,
15½ × 11⅞ in. (39.5 × 30 cm).
Peter Blum Collection, New York.

81. *Le Case si riempiono in cielo.* 1982.
(Houses Are Filling Themselves in the Sky)
Charcoal on paper,
15½ × 11⅞ in. (39.5 × 30 cm).
Peter Blum Collection, New York.

82. *Le case si riempiono d'aria.* 1982.
(Houses Are Filled with Air)
Poster sketch for the "Enzo Cucchi: Drawings" exhibition.
Zurich and Grongingen, 1982.
Two parts, each charcoal on paper,
each 16½ × 11⅝ in. (42 × 29.7 cm).
Groninger Museum, Groningen.

83. *Il pensiero della casa.* 1982.
(The Thought of the House)
Charcoal on paper,
11⅞ × 15¾ in. (30 × 40 cm).
Philipp Guyer Collection, St. Gallen.

84. *La casa cae sogna.* 1982.
(The House Dreams)
Charcoal on paper,
15½ × 11⅞ in. (39.5 × 30 cm).
Peter Blum Collection, New York.

85. *Il parto dell'ombra.* 1982.
(The Shadow Gives Birth)
Charcoal and pencil on paper,
15¾ × 11⅞ in. (40 × 30 cm).
Private collection.

86. *Il respiro della battaglia.* 1982.
(The Breath of Battle)
Charcoal on paper,
11⅞ × 15¾ in. (30 × 40 cm).
Private collection.

87. *L'anima nel paesaggio.* 1982.
(The Soul in the Landscape)
Charcoal, India ink and newspaper on paper,
15¾ × 11⅞ in. (40 × 30 cm).
Private collection.

88. *Viaggio della santa casa.* 1982.
(Journey of the Holy House)
India ink and pencil on paper,
15¾ × 11⅞ in. (40 × 30 cm).
Private collection.

89. *Die Berge widerstehen den Tieren.* 1982.
(The Mountains Oppose the Animals)
Pencil, charcoal, marking pen and white oil paint on grey paper,
17⅞ × 12 in. (45.5 × 30.5 cm).
Hamburger Kunsthalle, Hamburg.

90. *Untitled*. 1982.
India ink and pencil on paper,
15¾ × 11⅞ in. (40 × 30 cm).
Private collection.

91. *Il sogno di un giorno*. 1981-1982.
(The Dream of a Day)
Pencil, white wash and black and red India ink on paper,
11⅞ × 15½ in. (30 × 39.5 cm).
Peter Blum Collection, New York.

92. *Passeggiata della morte*. 1982.
(Death Promenade)
India ink, graphite and collage on paper,
12 × 15 in. (30.5 × 38.1 cm).
Private collection, United States.

93. *Un sogno ritrovato*. 1982.
(A Dream Recovered)
Pencil and charcoal on paper,
11⅞ × 15¾ in. (30 × 40 cm).
Private collection.

1983

94. *Untitled*. 1983.
Chalk on paper,
10½ × 8¼ in. (26.7 × 21 cm).
Peter Blum Collection, New York.

95. *Kolosseum zu: Giulio Cesare Roma*. 1983.
(Closed Coliseum: Julius Caesar Rome)
Photocopy and collage on cardboard,
16¾ × 18½ in. (42.5 × 47 cm).
Öffentliche Kunstsammlung,, Basle.
Hans-Jacob Oeri Donation, Basle.

96. *Giulio Cesare Roma*. 1983.
Charcoal on paper,
11¼ × 15¾ in. (28.5 × 40 cm).
Akira Ikeda Gallery, Tokyo.

97. *La vita è spaventata*. 1983.
(Life is Startled)
Watercolor and ink on paper,
12¾ × 9 in. (32.5 × 23 cm).
Private collection, Munich.

98. *I pensieri arrivano ancora*. 1983.
(Thoughts Are Still Arriving)
Watercolor and ink on paper,
12¾ × 9 in. (32.5 × 23 cm).
Private collection, Munich.

99. *Il ritratto di un pensiero*. 1983.
(The Portrait of a Thought)
Part of *La Scimmia* (The Simian), New York, 1983.
Graphite, India ink and collage on paper,
16½ × 13 in. (41.9 × 33 cm).
Julian Schnabel Collection, New York.

100. *Dei ed eroi*. 1983.
(Gods and Heroes)
Part of *La Scimmia*, New York, 1983.
Graphite, India ink and collage on paper,
25 × 19¼ in. (63.5 × 49 cm).
Private collection, United States.

101. *Untitled*. 1983.
Part of *La Scimmia*, New York, 1983.
Graphite on paper,
25¼ × 19½ in. (64.1 × 49.5 cm).
Caroline and Dick Anderson Collection, United States.

102. *Untitled*. 1983.
Part of *La Scimmia*, New York, 1983.
Graphite, India ink and collage on paper,
24½ × 19½ in. (62.2 × 49.5 cm).
Joshua L. Mack Collection, United States.

103. *Untitled.* 1983.
Part of *La Scimmia*, New York, 1983.
Graphite on paper,
25 × 20 in. (63.5 × 50.8 cm).
Private collection.

104. *Untitled.* 1983.
Part of *La Scimmia*, New York, 1983.
Graphite, India ink and collage on paper,
24½ × 19½ in. (62.2 × 49.5 cm).
PaineWebber Group Inc. Collection, New York.

105. *Circostanza.* 1983.
(Circumstances)
India ink, watercolor and collage on paper,
11⅝ × 12⅜ in. (29.5 × 31.5 cm).
Akira Ikeda Gallery, Tokyo.

106. *Paesaggio barbaro.* 1983.
(Barbaric Landscape)
Watercolor and collage on paper,
7⅝ × 13¾ in. (19.5 × 35 cm).
Akira Ikeda Gallery, Tokyo.

107. *Più vicino agli dei.* 1983.
(Closer to the Gods)
Black India ink, red ink and pencil on paper,
15½ × 11¾ in. (39.4 × 29.9 cm).
Staatliche Graphische Sammlung, Munich.

108. *Sperone.* 1983.
(Spur)
Black chalk on paper,
12⅝ × 9 in. (32 × 23 cm).
Private collection.

109. *Uno scherzo della natura.* 1983.
(One of Nature's Jokes)
Watercolor and pencil on paper,
15½ × 11⅞ in. (39.5 × 30 cm).
Galerie Yarlow/Salzman, Toronto.

110. *Il sogno del mare.* 1983.
(The Dream of the Sea)
Watercolor and collage on paper,
18½ × 13¾ in. (47 × 35 cm).
Galerie Bernd Klüser, Munich.

111. *Untitled.* 1983.
India ink, watercolor and collage on paper,
12⅝ × 8¼ in. (32.2 × 21.1 cm).
Franz Meyer Collection, Zurich.

112. *Il desiderio di un paesaggio.* 1983.
Watercolor and pencil on paper,
14⅛ × 10 in. (36 × 25.5 cm).
Akira Ikeda Gallery, Tokyo.

113. *Pasto cosmico.* 1983.
(Cosmic Food)
India ink, graphite, charcoal and white wash on paper,
16⅛ × 9⅞ in. (41 × 25 cm).
Prelinger Collection, Munich.

114. *Accanto allo spirito degli eroi.* 1983.
(Next to the Spirit of Heroes)
Black India ink, wash, white gouache and collage on paper,
18⅛ × 14 in. (46.2 × 35.6 cm).
Private collection.

115. *La fisarmonica della terra.* 1983.
(The Accordion of the Earth)
India ink and pencil on paper,
16 × 10 in. (940.5 × 25.5 cm).
Private collection.

116. *La ninna nanna della terra.* 1983.
(The Lullaby of the Earth)
Watercolor and pencil on paper,
14¾ × 11 in. (37.5 × 28 cm).
Akira Ikeda Gallery, Tokyo.

117. *Untitled.* 1983.
Pencil and India ink on paper,
15⅛ × 11⅞ in. (38.5 × 30 cm).
Galerie Bruno Bischofberger, Zurich.

118. *Giulio Cesare Roma.* 1983.
Charcoal on paper,
18¾ × 14 in. (47.5 × 35.5 cm).
Akira Ikeda Gallery, Tokyo.

119. *Untitled.* 1983.
Charcoal and pencil on paper,
8⅜ × 10½ in. (21.2 × 26.5 cm).
Franz Meyer Collection, Zurich.

120. *Untitled.* 1983.
Charcoal and ballpoint on paper,
8⅜ × 10¼ in. (21.2 × 26 cm).
Franz Meyer Collection, Zurich.

121. *Untitled.* 1983.
Pencil, charcoal and green ballpoint on paper,
11⅜ × 15½ in. (29 × 39.5 cm).
Private collection.

122. *Untitled.* 1983.
(Pianist)
Pencil and cardboard on paper,
8½ × 8⅜ in. (21.6 × 21.3 cm).
Kupferstichkabinett,
Öffentliche Kunstsammlung, Basle.
Hans-Jakob Oeri Donation, Basle.

123. *Girotondo della vita.* 1983.
(Circle of Life)
Pencil and charcoal on paper,
12¾ × 16⅛ in. (32.5 × 41 cm).
Akira Ikeda Gallery, Tokyo.

124. *Untitled.* 1983
Pencil and charcoal on paper,
12⅝ × 17¼ in. (32 × 43.7 cm).
Private collection.

125. *Giulio Cesare Roma.* 1983.
Charcoal on paper,
11 × 15¾ in. (27.7 × 40 cm).
Akira Ikeda Gallery, Tokyo.

126. *Untitled.* 1983.
Pencil on paper,
8⅜ × 10½ in. (21.2 × 26.8 cm).
Private collection.

127. *Gli alberi respirano con gli animali.* 1983.
(The Trees Breathe With the Animals)
Pencil and charcoal on paper,
15¾ × 11⅞ in. (40 × 30 cm).
Galerie Bruno Bischofberger, Zurich.

1984

128. *Untitled.* 1984.
Part of *Tetto* (Roof).
Charcoal on paper,
6¼ × 9¼ in. (16 × 23.5 cm).
Galerie Bruno Bischofberger, Zurich.

129. *Untitled.* 1984.
Pencil on paper,
13½ × 18⅛ in. (34.5 × 46 cm).
Courtesy of Bruno Bischofberger, Zurich.

130. *Untitled.* 1984.
Black chalk on paper,
10¼ × 18¼ in. (26.2 × 46.5 cm).
Peter Degermark Collection,
United States.

131. *Untitled.* 1984.
Part of *Italia.*
Pencil, chalk and charcoal on paper,
17¼ × 7⅛ in. (43.9 × 18.1 cm).
Art Gallery of South Australia, Adelaide.

132. *Untitled.* 1984.
Part of *Tetto* (Roof).
Charcoal on paper,
18⅛ × 7 in. (46 × 18 cm).
Silvana Stipa Collection, Rome.

133. *Pesce predicatore.* 1984.
(Preacher Fish)
Chalk and pencil on paper,
7½ × 14¾ in. (19 × 37.5 cm).
Joshua L. Mack Collection,
United States.

134. *La casa gravida*. 1984.
(The Pregnant House)
Pencil on paper,
17¼ × 6¾ in. (44 × 17 cm).
Courtesy of Galerie Ascan Crone, Hamburg.

135. *Untitled*. 1984.
Black chalk on paper,
11⅞ × 15¾ in. (30 × 40 cm).
Private collection, United States.

136. *Untitled*. 1984.
Black chalk on paper,
12⅝ × 9½ in. (32 × 24 cm).
Private collection, London.

137. *Ultimo eroe*. 1984.
(Last Hero)
Pencil on paper,
6¾ × 17¼ in. (17 × 44 cm).
Courtesy of Galerie Ascan Crone, Hamburg.

138. *Untitled*. 1984.
Pencil, black chalk and watercolor on paper,
16⅛ × 7 in. (41 × 18 cm).
Private collection, London.

139. *Untitled*. 1984.
Pencil on paper,
7⅞ × 9½ in. (20 × 24 cm).
Joshua L. Mack Collection, United States.

140. *Untitled (Vitebsk-Harar)*. 1984.
India ink on paper,
12 × 14 in. (30.5 × 35.6 cm).
Joshua L. Mack Collection, United States.

141. *Vitebsk-Harar*. 1984.
India ink on paper,
118¼ × 15¼ in. (46.4 × 38.7 cm).
Private collection, London.

142. *Untitled (Vitebsk-Harar)*. 1984.
Ballpoint on paper,
3¾ × 5⅞ in. (9.4 × 15 cm).
Galerie Bruno Bischofberger, Zurich.

143. *Harar*. 1984.
India ink and marker on paper,
15 × 16 in. (38.1 × 40.6 cm).
Galerie Sperone Westwater, New York.

144. *Vitebsk-Harar*. 1984.
India ink on paper,
9½ × 5½ in. (24.1 × 14 cm).
Joshua L. Mack Collection, United States.

145. *Untitled (Vitebsk-Harar)*. 1984.
Black chalk on paper,
7⅞ × 7⅞ in. (20 × 20 cm).
Compagnia del Disegno, Milan.

146. *Untitled (Vitebsk-Harar)*. 1984.
Pencil on paper,
5½ × 16 in. (14.2 × 40.6 cm).
Private collection, United States.

147. *Untitled*. 1984.
Pencil on paper,
9½ × 11⅞ in. (24 × 30 cm).
Galerie Bernd Klüser, Munich.

148. *Il veleno delle sculture*. 1984.
(The Poison of Sculptures)
Ballpoint on cardboard,
8⅝ × 7⅞ in. (22 × 20 cm).
Private collection, Munich.

149. *Il veleno delle sculture*. 1984.
(The Poison of Sculptures)
Ballpoint on cardboard,
8⅝ × 7⅞ in. (22 × 20 cm).
Private collection, Munich.

150. *Untitled*. 1984.
Pencil on paper,
14⅛ × 18⅞ in. (36 × 48 cm.)
Private collection, Munich.

151. *Untitled*. 1984.
Pencil on paper,
14⅛ × 18⅞ in. (36 × 48 cm).
Private collection, Munich.

152. *Untitled*. 1984.
Pencil on paper,
9½ × 11⅞ in. (24 × 30 cm).
Galerie Bernd Klüser, Munich.

153. *Untitled*. 1984.
Pencil on paper,
14⅛ × 18⅞ in. (36 × 48 cm).
Private collection.

154. *Untitled*. 1984.
Sheet 1 of the group of 4 drawings
Skulptur für Basel.
(Sculpture for Basle)
India ink on paper,
6¼ × 9½ in. (16 × 24 cm).
Private collection, Munich.

155. *Untitled*. 1984.
Sheet 2 of the group of 4 drawings
Skulptur für Basel.
India ink on paper,
10¼ × 9½ in. (26 × 24 cm).
Private collection, Munich.

156. *Untitled*. 1984.
Sheet 3 of the group of 4 drawings
Skulptur für Basel.
India ink on paper,
6¼ × 9½ in. (16 × 24 cm).
Private collection, Munich.

157. *Untitled*. 1984.
Sheet 4 of the group of 4 drawings
Skulptur für Basel.
India ink on paper,
6¼ × 9½ in. (16 × 24 cm).
Private collection, Munich.

1985

158. *Untitled*. 1985
Part of *34 disegni cantano I*, 1.
(34 Drawings Sing I, 1)
Charcoal and ballpoint on torn cardboard,
8¼ × 6¾ in. (20.9 × 17.2 cm).
Private collection, Munich.

159. *Untitled*. 1984-1985.
Part of *34 disegni cantano I*, 12.
Ballpoint on paper,
4 × 6 in. (10.1 × 15.2 cm).
Courtesy of the Galerie Harald Behm, Hamburg.

160. *Untitled*. 1984-1985.
Part of *34 disegni cantano I*, 8.
Ballpoint on paper,
9⅜ × 4½ in. (23.7 × 11.5 cm).
Kunstmuseum Düsseldorf, Dusseldorf.

161. *Untitled*. 1984-1985.
Part of *34 disegni cantano II*, 3.
Ballpoint on paper,
4⅜ × 4 in. (11 × 10.2 cm).
Galerie Rudolf Zwirner, Cologne.

162. *Untitled*. 1984-1985.
Part of *34 disegni cantano I*, 4.
Ballpoint on paper,
4 × 6 in. (10.1 × 15.2 cm).
Galeria Daniel Varenne, Geneva.

163. *Untitled*. 1985.
Part of *34 disegni cantano I*, 3.
Ballpoint on cardboard,
4½ × 7 in. (11.5 × 17.5 cm).
Kunstmuseum Düsseldorf, Dusseldorf.

164. *Untitled*. 1984-1985.
Part of *34 disegni cantano I*, 5.
Ballpoint on paper,
4 × 6 in. (10.2 × 15.2 cm).
Galerie Daniel Varenne, Geneva.

165. *Untitled.* 1984-1985.
Part of *34 disegni cantano II*, 5.
Ballpoint on paper,
5½ × 8⅝ in. (14 × 22 cm).
Galerie Bernd Klüser, Munich.

166. *Untitled.* 1984-1985.
Part of *34 disegni cantano I*, 7.
Ballpoint on paper,
4 × 6 in. (10.1 × 15.2 cm).
Courtesy of Galerie Harald Behm, Hamburg.

167. *Untitled.* 1984-1985.
Part of *34 disegni cantano I*, 11.
Pencil and charcoal on torn paper,
6⅝ × 8½ in. (16.8 × 21.7 cm).
Galerie Daniel Varenne, Geneva.

168. *Untitled.* 1984-1985.
Part of *34 disegni cantano I*, 10.
Pencil and charcoal on torn paper,
7¼ × 10⅛ in. (18.4 × 25.7 cm).
Kunstmuseum Düsseldorf, Dusseldorf.

169. *Untitled.* 1984-1985.
Part of *34 disegni cantano I*, 2.
Pencil and charcoal on torn paper,
4 × 16⅞ in. (10 × 42.8 cm).
Kunstmuseum Düsseldorf, Dusseldorf.

170. *Untitled.* 1984-1985.
Part of *34 disegni cantano II*, 7.
Ballpoint on paper,
5½ × 8⅝ in. (14 × 22 cm).
Private collection.

171. *Untitled.* 1984-1985.
Part of *34 disegni cantano II*, 8.
Ballpoint on paper,
5⅜ × 6⅞ in. (13.7 × 17.3 cm).
Galerie Bernd Klüser, Munich.

172. *Untitled.* 1984-1985.
Part of *34 disegni cantano II*, 2.
Ballpoint on cardboard,
4½ × 7 in. (11.5 × 17.5 cm).
Kunstmuseum Düsseldorf, Dusseldorf.

173. *Untitled.* 1984-1985.
Part of *34 disegni cantano II*, 16.
Ballpoint on paper,
4½ × 7 in. (11.5 × 17.5 cm).
Vivian Horan Gallery, New York.

174. *Untitled.* 1985.
Part of *34 disegni cantano I*, 15.
Ballpoint on paper,
5½ × 7⅜ in. (14 × 18.8 cm).
Galerie Bernd Klüser, Munich.

175. *Untitled.* 1985.
Part of *34 disegni cantano I*, 16.
Ballpoint on paper,
8⅝ × 4 in. (21.9 × 10 cm).
Galerie Rudolf Zwirner, Cologne.

176. *Untitled.* 1984-1985.
Part of *34 disegni cantano I*, 13.
Ballpoint on paper,
4 × 6 in. (10.1 × 15.2 cm).
Galerie Bernd Klüser, Munich.

177. *Untitled.* 1984-1985.
Part of *34 disegni cantano I*, 14.
Pencil and India ink on paper,
9¼ × 12½ in. (23.4 × 31.9 cm).
Private collection, Munich.

178. *Untitled.* 1985.
Part of *34 disegni cantano II*, 1.
Ballpoint and India ink on paper,
5½ × 8⅝ in. (14 × 22 cm).
Private collection, Munich.

179. *Untitled.* 1984-1985.
Part of *34 disegni cantano II*, 4.
Ballpoint on paper,
4½ × 7 in. (11.5 × 17.5 cm).
Galerie Bernd Klüser, Munich.

180. *Untitled.* 1985.
Part of 34 disegni cantano II, 11.
Ballpoint on paper,
5⅜ × 6⅞ in. (13.7 × 17.3 cm).
Private collection, Munich.

181. *Untitled.* 1985.
Part of *34 disegni cantano II*, 12.
Ballpoint on paper,
5⅜ × 6⅞ in. (13.7 × 17.3 cm).
Private collection, Solothurn.

182. *Untitled.* 1984-1985.
Part of *34 disegni cantano II*, 10.
Ballpoint on paper,
5½ × 8⅝ in. (14 × 22 cm).
Galerie Rudolf Zwirner, Cologne.

183. *Untitled.* 1984-1985.
Part of *34 disegni cantano II*, 15.
Ballpoint on paper,
5½ × 7⅞ in. (14 × 19.9 cm).
Galerie Rudolf Zwirner, Cologne.

184. *Untitled.* 1985.
Part of *34 disegni cantano II*, 17.
Ballpoint on paper,
5½ × 8⅝ in. (14 × 22 cm).
Private collection, Munich.

185. *Untitled.* 1985.
Part of *34 disegni cantano II*, 14.
Ballpoint on paper,
5½ × 8⅝ in. (14 × 22 cm).
Galerie Rudolf Zwirner, Cologne.

186. *Untitled.* 1985.
Part of *34 disegni cantano II*, 15.
Ballpoint on paper,
8 × 5½ in. (20.2 × 14 cm).
Private collection, Munich.

187. *Untitled.* 1985.
Black chalk on paper,
5⅞ × 9¼ in. (15 × 23.5 cm).
Galerie Michael Haas, Berlin.

188. *Untitled.* 1985.
Charcoal on paper,
9⅞ × 8½ in. (25 × 21.6 cm).
Courtesy of Galerie Anthony d'Offay, London.

189. *Untitled.* 1985.
Wax crayon and pencil on paper,
9 × 8⅝ in. (23 × 22 cm).
Galerie Bruno Bischofberger, Zurich.

190. *Untitled.* 1985.
Charcoal and pencil on paper,
7 × 9½ in. (18 × 24 cm).
Galerie Bruno Bischofberger, Zurich.

191. *Untitled.* 1985.
Black chalk on paper,
10⅝ × 8½ in. (27 × 21.6 cm).
Raymond J. Learsy Collection, United States.

192. *Untitled.* 1985.
Black chalk on paper,
10⅝ × 8½ in. (27 × 21.6 cm).
Raymond J. Learsy Collection, United States.

193. *Untitled.* 1985.
Preparatory sketch for the cement painting for the Guggenheim exhibition, 1986.
4 × 2⅜ in. (10 × 6 cm).
Galerie Michael Haas, Berlin.

194. *Untitled.* 1985.
Preparatory sketch for the cement painting for the Guggenheim exhibition, 1986.
India ink on paper,
3½ × 2½ in. (9 × 6.5 cm).

195. *Untitled.* 1985.
Black chalk on paper,
7 × 9⅝ in. (18 × 24.5 cm).
Galerie Michael Haas, Berlin.

196. *Untitled.* 1985.
Pencil and black wash on paper,
15½ × 11⅞ in. (39.6 × 30 cm).
Private collection.

197. *Untitled.* 1985.
Pencil on paper,
5⅞ × 9¼ in. (15 × 23.5 cm).
Galerie Michael Haas, Berlin.

198. *Harar, A.R.* 1985.
Pencil on paper,
9⅜ × 6¼ in. (23.8 × 16 cm).
Peter Blum Collection, New York.

199. *Untitled.* 1985.
Pencil and charcoal on cardboard,
6¼ × 9½ in. (16 × 24 cm).
Private collection, Madrid.

200. *Untitled* (*Solchi d'Europa*). 1985.
(Furrows of Europe)
Ballpoint and charcoal on paper,
7¼ × 3¾ in. (18.5 × 9.5 cm).
Private collection, Munich.

201. *Untitled.* 1985.
Black chalk on paper,
7 × 9⅝ in. (18 × 24.5 cm).
Galerie Michael Haas, Berlin.

202. *Untitled.* 1985.
Charcoal and India ink on paper,
6¼ × 9½ in. (16 × 24 cm).
Private collection, United States.

203. *Untitled.* 1985.
Pencil on paper,
7 × 9⅝ in. (18 × 24.5 cm).
Private collection, Madrid.

204. *Harar.* 1985.
India ink and wash on cardboard,
6¼ × 4⅜ in. (16 × 11 cm).
Courtesy of Christine Lalou, Paris.

205. *Harar, A.R.* 1985.
India ink and ballpoint on paper,
6¼ × 4⅜ in. (16 × 11 cm).
Peter Blum Collection, New York.

206. *La stanza del fiato.* 1985.
(The Hall of Breath)
India ink and wash on paper,
6¼ × 4⅜ in. (16 × 11 cm).
Courtesy of Galerie Daniel Templon, Paris.

207. *Untitled.* 1985.
Part of *Solchi d'Europa.*
Indian ink on paper,
4⅜ × 6¼ in. (11 × 16 cm).
Mancini Collection, Pesaro.

208. *Untitled.* 1985.
Part of *Solchi d'Europa.*
India ink on paper,
4 × 6½ in. (10 × 16.5 cm).
Mancini Collection, Pesaro.

209. *Untitled.* 1985.
Part of *Solchi d'Europa.*
Charcoal on paper,
9¼ × 6¼ in. (23.5 × 16 cm).
Mancini Collection, Pesaro.

210. *Untitled.* 1985.
Part of *Solchi d'Europa.*
Charcoal on paper,
6¾ × 7½ in. (17 × 19 cm).
Mancini Collection, Pesaro.

211. *Untitled.* 1985.
Part of *Solchi d'Europa.*
Pencil and charcoal on paper,
9⅜ × 6 in. (23.7 × 15.2 cm).
Prelinger Collection, Munich.

212. *Untitled.* 1985.
Charcoal on paper,
5 × 7½ in. (12.5 × 19 cm).
Private collection, Grünwald.

213. *Untitled.* 1985.
Part of *Solchi d'Europa.*
Charcoal on paper,
5 × 7½ in. (12.5 × 19 cm).
Galerie Bernd Klüser, Munich.

214. *Untitled.* 1985.
Part of *Solchi d'Europa.*
Charcoal and paper,
4¾ × 6¼ in. (12 × 16 cm).
Private collection, Munich.

215. *Untitled*. 1985.
Part of *Solchi d'Europa*.
Charcoal on paper,
6¼ × 9½ in. (16 × 24 cm).
Courtesy of Galerie Harald Behm, Hamburg.

1986

216. *Untitled*. 1986.
India ink on paper,
4⅝ × 7 in. (11.7 × 17.5 cm).
Courtesy of Sperone Westwater Gallery, New York.

217. *Untitled*. 1986.
Charcoal and pencil on paper,
9¼ × 12⅜ in. (23.5 × 31.4 cm).
Private collection.

218. *Untitled*. 1986.
Charcoal and pencil on paper,
11½ × 12¾ in. (29.2 × 31.8 cm).
Private collection, New York.

219. *Untitled*. 1986.
Pencil, chalk and charcoal on paper,
14⅛ × 6½ in. (35.9 × 16.5 cm).
Private collection, Stockholm.

220. *Untitled*. 1986.
Pencil and wax crayon on paper,
12¼ × 5⅝ in. (31.1 × 14.3 cm).
Private collection, New York.

221. *Untitled*. 1986.
Black chalk on paper,
6 × 17 in. (15.2 × 43.2 cm).
Galerie Michael Haas, Berlin.

222. *Untitled*. 1986.
Pencil and charcoal on paper,
8 × 14¼ in. (20.3 × 36.2 cm).
Sperone Westwater Gallery, New York.

223. *Untitled*. 1986.
Pencil and brown pencil on paper, with cardboard support,
12⅜ × 6⅞ in. (31.3 × 17.5 cm).
Galerie Bruno Bischofberger, Zurich.

224. *Untitled*. 1986.
Charcoal, pencil and chalk on paper,
8 × 18⅛ in. (20.3 × 46 cm).
Kunsthaus Zürich, Graphische Sammlung, Zurich.

225. *Untitled*. 1986.
Pencil, chalk and India ink on paper,
9 × 13 in. (22.9 × 33 cm).
Kunsthaus Zürich, Graphische Sammlung, Zurich.

226. *Untitled*. 1986.
India ink, charcoal and pencil on paper,
6⅝ × 9½ in. (16.8 × 24.1 cm).
M. Anwar Kamal Collection, United States.

227. *Untitled*. 1986.
Charcoal, chalk and pencil on paper,
10⅝ × 8½ in. (27 × 21.6 cm).
Private collection.

228. *Untitled*. 1986.
Pencil and India ink on paper,
5⅞ × 14¼ in. (14.9 × 36.2 cm).
Sperone Westwater Gallery, New York.

229. *Untitled*. 1986.
Chalk and charcoal on paper,
6⅛ × 18⅛ in. (15.6 × 46 cm).
Private collection, United States.

230. *Untitled*. 1986.
Pencil on paper,
6⅛ × 18⅛ in. (15.6 × 46 cm).
Private collection.

231. *Untitled*. 1986.
Charcoal, chalk and pencil on paper,
10⅝ × 8½ in. (27 × 21.6 cm).
Private collection, United States.

232. *Untitled*. 1986.
Pencil and charcoal on paper,
10⅝ × 8½ in. (27 × 21.4 cm).
Private collection, Basle.

233. *Untitled*. 1986.
Pencil and India ink on paper,
6 × 13 in. (15.2 × 33 cm).
Private collection, Los Angeles.

234. *Untitled*. 1986.
Pencil, wax crayon and charcoal
on paper,
6⅛ × 18⅛ in. (15.6 × 46 cm).
Private collection.

235. *Untitled*. 1986.
Charcoal and pencil on paper,
5⅝ × 18¾ in. (13.7 × 47.5 cm).
Peter Blum Collection, New York.

236. *Untitled*. 1986.
Charcoal and pencil on paper,
6⅜ × 19⅞ in. (16.3 × 47.8 cm).
Peter Blum Collection, New York.

237. *Untitled*. 1986.
Charcoal and chalk on paper,
10⅝ × 8½ in. (27 × 21.6 cm).
Private collection, United States.

238. *Untitled*. 1986.
Charcoal, pencil and chalk on paper,
8½ × 10¾ in. (21.5 × 27.4 cm).
Peter Blum Collection, New York.

239. *Untitled*. 1986.
Pencil and wax crayon on paper,
6⅛ × 18⅛ in. (15.6 × 46 cm).
Private collection.

240. *Untitled*. 1986.
India ink and ballpoint on paper,
2⅞ × 8½ in. (7.3 × 21.5 cm).
Galerie Michael Haas, Berlin.

241. *Untitled*. 1986.
Ink and collage on painted paper,
4¾ × 10 in. (12 × 25.5 cm).
Peter Blum Collection, New York.

242. *Untitled*. 1986.
India ink on paper,
9 × 3¼ in. (22.9 × 8.3 cm).
Galerie Michael Haas, Berlin.

243. *Untitled*. 1986.
Pencil and chalk on paper,
9¼ × 14¼ in. (23.5 × 36.2 cm).
Private collection, New York.

244. *Untitled*. 1986.
Pencil, wax crayon, chalk and India ink
on paper,
8⅞ × 11 in. (22.5 × 27.9 cm).
Private collection.

245. *Untitled*. 1986.
Charcoal and pencil on paper,
5⅛ × 18⅞ in. (13 × 47.8 cm).
Peter Blum Collection, New York.

246. *Untitled*. 1986.
Charcoal, chalk and India ink on paper,
6¼ × 18⅛ in. (15.9 × 46 cm).
PaineWebber Group Inc. Collection,
New York.

247. *Untitled*. 1986.
Ink and pencil on cardboard,
11½ × 5½ in. (29.2 × 14 cm).
Courtesy of Galerie Ascan Crone,
Hamburg.

248. *Untitled*. 1986.
Pencil and wax crayon on paper,
11 × 8¾ in. (27.9 × 22.2 cm).
Private collection, New York.

249. *Untitled*. 1986.
Charcoal and chalk on paper,
$6\frac{3}{4} \times 9\frac{1}{2}$ in. (17×24 cm).
Galerie Bruno Bischofberger, Zurich.

250. *Untitled*. 1986.
Ballpoint and India ink on paper,
$8\frac{1}{8} \times 10$ in. (20.6×25.2 cm).
Private collection, Switzerland.

251. *Untitled*. 1986.
Pencil and wax crayon on paper,
$4\frac{7}{8} \times 9\frac{1}{2}$ in. (12.2×24 cm).
Galerie Bernd Klüser, Munich.

252. *Untitled*. 1986.
Pencil on paper,
$8\frac{1}{4} \times 8$ in. (21.1×20.5 cm).
Galerie Bernd Klüser, Munich.

1987

253. *Untitled*. 1987.
Pencil and India ink on paper,
$9\frac{1}{2} \times 6\frac{1}{2}$ in. (24×16.6 cm).
Galerie Bruno Bischofberger, Zurich.

254. *Untitled*. 1987.
Ballpoint and marker on cardboard,
$4\frac{5}{8} \times 6\frac{1}{4}$ in. (11.9×15.9 cm).
Galerie Bernd Klüser, Munich.

255. *Untitled*. 1987.
Ballpoint and ink on paper,
$6\frac{1}{2} \times 9\frac{1}{2}$ in. (16.5×24 cm).
Compagnia del Disegno, Milan.

256. *Untitled*. 1987.
Chalk and charcoal on paper,
$9\frac{1}{2} \times 9\frac{7}{8}$ in. (24×25 cm).
Compagnia del Disegno, Milan.

257. *Untitled*. 1987.
Ballpoint on paper,
$6\frac{3}{4} \times 5$ in. (17×12.5 cm).
Private collection, Switzerland.

258. *Untitled*. 1987.
Ballpoint on paper,
$5\frac{1}{4} \times 7\frac{1}{8}$ in. (13.3×18.2 cm).
Galerie Bernd Klüser, Munich.

259. *Untitled*. 1987.
Ballpoint and marker on cardboard,
$6\frac{5}{8} \times 4\frac{1}{2}$ in. (16.8×11.4 cm).
Courtesy of Galerie Bernd Klüser, Munich.

260. *Untitled*. 1987.
Pencil, India ink and blue ballpoint
on white and yellow paper,
with mirror collage,
$7\frac{1}{4} \times 9\frac{1}{2}$ in. (18.5×24 cm).
Compagnia del Disegno, Milan.

261. *Untitled*. 1987.
Pencil on cardboard,
$6\frac{1}{4} \times 8\frac{7}{8}$ in. (16×22.5 cm).
Compagnia del Disegno, Milan.

262. *Untitled*. 1987.
Ballpoint and pencil on paper,
$6\frac{1}{2} \times 9\frac{1}{2}$ in. (16.5×24 cm).
Compagnia del Disegno, Milan.

263. *Untitled*. 1987.
India ink and violet and
red ballpoints on paper, with
mirror collage,
$4\frac{5}{8} \times 6\frac{1}{4}$ in. (11.9×15.9 cm).
Galerie Bernd Klüser, Munich.

264. *Untitled*. 1987.
Ballpoint on paper,
$4\frac{7}{8} \times 3\frac{1}{4}$ in. (12.4×8.4 cm).
Private collection, Switzerland.

265. *Untitled*. 1987.
Pencil, charcoal and India ink on paper,
$7 \times 8\frac{5}{8}$ in. (917.7×22 cm).
Private collection, Basle.

266. *Untitled*. 1987.
Ballpoint and collage on paper and mirror,
$5\frac{3}{4} \times 11\frac{1}{2}$ in. (14.7×29.3 cm).
Private collection, Basle.

267. *Untitled*. 1987.
India ink and ballpoint on yellow paper, 4 × 5¼ in. (910.3 × 13.4 cm).
Kunstsammlung der Basler Versicherungs-Gesellschaft, Basle.

268. *Untitled*. 1987.
Ballpoint and marker on paper, 5⅞ × 8¼ in. (15 × 20.9 cm).
Private collection, Munich.

269. *Untitled*. 1987.
Ballpoint and marker on paper, 6¼ × 8 in. (16 × 20.5 cm).
Private collection, Munich.

270. *Untitled*. 1987.
Ballpoint, India ink and mirror on paper,
8⅜ × 5¾ in. (21 × 14.5 cm).
Z. Mis Collection, Brussels.

271. *Untitled*. 1987.
Blue and black ballpoints and India ink on paper,
4½ × 4½ in. (11.5 × 11.5 cm).
Private collection.

272. *Untitled*. 1987.
Ballpoint on cardboard,
4⅜ × 6¼ in. (11 × 16 cm).
Private collection, Munich.

273. *Fontana vista*. 1987.
(Fountain Seen)
Pencil on paper,
12¼ × 8¾ in. (31 × 22.3 cm).
Private collection, Munich.

274. *Untitled*. 1987.
Pencil, charcoal, India ink, ballpoint and collage on paper,
9½ × 15⅞ in. (24 × 32 cm).
Private collection, Basle.

275. *Untitled*. 1987.
Ink on paper,
7⅛ × 9½ in. (18.1 × 24 cm).
Galerie Bernd Klüser, Munich.

276. *Untitled*. 1987.
Ballpoint on paper,
46 × 9½ in. (116.6 × 23.9 cm).
Galerie Bernd Klüser, Munich.

277. *Untitled*. 1987.
Ballpoint and marker on cardboard,
4½ × 2⅝ in. (11.4 × 16.8 cm).
Galerie Bernd Klüser, Munich.

278. *Untitled*. 1987.
Pencil, ink and wax crayon on paper,
7 × 9½ in. (17.4 × 24.1 cm).
Akira Ikeda Gallery, Tokyo.

279. *Untitled no. 7*. 1987.
Ink, watercolor, wax crayon and collage on paper,
7¼ × 9½ in. (18.5 × 24 cm).
Akira Ikeda Gallery, Tokyo.

280. *Untitled*. 1987.
Pencil and ballpoint on paper,
6¾ × 9½ in. (17 × 23.9 cm).
Galerie Bernd Klüser, Munich.

281. *Untitled*. 1987.
Ballpoint on cardboard,
3¾ × 4½ in. (9.7 × 11.7 cm).
Galerie Bernd Klüser, Munich.

282. *Untitled no. 1*. 1987.
Ink on paper,
8 × 5⅜ in. (20.5 × 13.7 cm).
Akira Ikeda Gallery, Tokyo.

283. *Untitled no. 6*. 1987.
Pencil, ink and wax crayon on paper,
9 × 7⅛ in. (23 × 18.1 cm).
Akira Ikeda Gallery, Tokyo.

284. *Luc'é*. 1987.
Pencil on yellowish reinforced paper,
$11\frac{1}{2} \times 8\frac{3}{8}$ in. (29.5 × 21.2 cm).
Klüser Collection, Munich.

1988

285. *Untitled*. 1988.
Pencil and wax crayon on paper,
$24\frac{1}{2} \times 5\frac{3}{4}$ in. (62 × 14.5 cm).
Galerie Bruno Bischofberger, Zurich.

286. *Untitled*. 1988.
Pencil on paper,
$6\frac{1}{8} \times 8\frac{1}{2}$ in. (15.7 × 21.6 cm).
The artist's collection.

287. *Untitled*. 1988.
Pencil on paper,
$4\frac{1}{2} \times 6\frac{5}{8}$ in. (11.5 × 16.9 cm).
The artist's collection.

288. *Untitled*. 1988.
Pencil on paper.
$8\frac{1}{8} \times 6\frac{1}{8}$ in. (20.7 × 15.7 cm).
The artist's collection.

289. *Untitled*. 1988.
Pencil on paper,
$7 \times 9\frac{7}{8}$ in. (17.5 × 25 cm).
The artist's collection.

290. *Untitled*. 1988.
Pencil on paper,
$7\frac{1}{2} \times 6\frac{1}{2}$ in. (19 × 16.5 cm).
The artist's collection.

291. *Untitled*. 1988.
Pencil on paper,
$8\frac{1}{4} \times 7$ in. (21 × 17.5 cm).
The artist's collection.

292. *Untitled*. 1988.
Pencil on paper,
$8\frac{1}{4} \times 5\frac{1}{4}$ in. (21 × 13.4 cm).
The artist's collection.

293. *Untitled*. 1988.
Pencil on paper,
$5\frac{7}{8} \times 8\frac{1}{8}$ in. (15 × 20.7 cm).
The artist's collection.

294. *Untitled*. 1988.
India ink on paper,
$3\frac{1}{8} \times 3\frac{7}{8}$ in. (7.9 × 9.8 cm).
The artist's collection.

295. *Untitled*. 1988.
Pencil on reinforced paper,
$5\frac{7}{8} \times 8\frac{1}{8}$ in. (14.8 × 20.8 cm).
Galerie Bernd Klüser, Munich.

296. *Untitled*. 1988.
Pencil and marker on paper,
$7 \times 9\frac{3}{4}$ in. (17.4 × 24.9 cm).
Galerie Bernd Klüser, Munich.

297. *Untitled*. 1988.
Pencil on paper,
$18\frac{7}{8} \times 10$ in. (48 × 25.3 cm).
Galerie Bernd Klüser, Munich.

298. *Untitled*. 1988.
Pencil, ink and wax crayon on paper,
$7 \times 9\frac{7}{8}$ in. (17.5 × 25 cm).
Akira Ikeda Gallery, Tokyo.

299. *Untitled*. 1988.
Pencil and ink on paper,
$4\frac{5}{8} \times 5\frac{1}{2}$ in. (11.8 × 14 cm).
Akira Ikeda Gallery, Tokyo.

300. *Untitled*. 1988.
Pencil and wax crayon on paper,
$7\frac{1}{8} \times 9\frac{5}{8}$ in. (18.1 × 24.5 cm).
Akira Ikeda Gallery, Tokyo.

301. *Untitled*. 1988.
Pencil and wax crayon on paper,
$7\frac{1}{8} \times 9\frac{1}{2}$ in. (18.1 × 24.2 cm).
Akira Ikeda Gallery, Tokyo.

302. *Untitled*. 1988.
Pencil on paper,
5⅝ × 5⅞ in. (914.3 × 15 cm).
Galerie Bernd Klüser, Munich.

303. *Untitled*. 1988.
Pencil, ink and wax crayon on paper,
6⅜ × 10¼ in. (16.2 × 26 cm).
Akira Akeda Gallery, Tokyo.

304. *Untitled*. 1988.
Ink and pencil on paper,
3 × 9 in. (7.6 × 23 cm).
Akira Akeda Gallery, Tokyo.

305. *Untitled*. 1988.
Pencil and ballpoint on paper,
8¼ × 5¼ in. (20.8 × 13.4 cm).
Galerie Bernd Klüser, Munich.

306. *Untitled*. 1988.
Pencil and ink on paper,
5⅝ × 9⅞ in. (14.2 × 25 cm).
Akira Ikeda Gallery, Tokyo.

307. *Untitled*. 1988.
Pencil on paper,
5¾ × 9⅛ in. (14.7 × 23.2 cm).
Galerie Bernd Klüser, Munich.

308. *Untitled*. 1988.
Pencil on paper,
8 × 20⅜ in. (20.4 × 52.5 cm).
Galerie Bernd Klüser, Munich.

309. *Untitled*. 1988.
Pencil on paper,
7⅛ × 5¾ in. (18.1 × 14.6 cm).
Klüser Collection, Munich.

310. *Untitled*. 1988.
Ink and pencil on paper,
6¾ × × 6 in. (17 × 15.3 cm).
Akira Ikeda Gallery, Tokyo.

311. *Untitled*. 1988.
Pencil on yellow paper,
7 × 9⅞ in. (17.5 × 25 cm).
Galerie Bernd Klüser, Munich.

312. *Untitled*. 1988.
Blue and green ballpoints on paper,
4½ × 6⅝ in. (11.5 × 16.9 cm).
Klüser Collection, Munich.

313. *Untitled*. 1988.
Pencil on paper,
8⅜ × 6¾ in. (21.3 × 17 cm).
Galerie Bernd Klüser, Munich.

314. *Untitled*. 1988.
Pencil on paper,
9⅝ × 7 in. (24.6 × 17.5 cm).
Galerie Bernd Klüser, Munich.

315. *Untitled*. 1988.
Ballpoint on paper,
5¾ × 3½ in. (14.7 × 9 cm).
Galerie Bernd Klüser, Munich.

316. *Untitled*. 1988.
Black ballpoint on paper,
8⅛ × 5⅜ in. (20.8 × 13.5 cm).
Galerie Bernd Klüser, Munich.

317. *Untitled*. 1988.
Black ballpoint and India ink on squared paper,
6 × 4 in. (15.2 × 10.4 cm).
Galerie Bernd Klüser, Munich.

318. *Untitled*. 1988.
Black ballpoint on grey-brown paper,
5⅛ × 7¾ in. (13.2 × 19.6 cm).
Galerie Bernd Klüser, Munich.

319. *Untitled*. 1988.
Red and black ballpoints on paper,
4¼ × 3⅜ in. (10.9 × 8.5 cm).
Galerie Bernd Klüser, Munich.

320. *Untitled.* 1988.
Red ballpoint on squared paper,
3⅜ × 6 in. (10.4 × 15.2 cm).
Galerie Bernd Klüser, Munich.

321. *Untitled.* 1988.
Red ballpoint on grey-brown paper,
5¾ × 7⅝ in. (14.5 × 19.4 cm).
Galerie Bernd Klüser, Munich.

322. *Untitled.* 1988.
Black ballpoint on reinforced paper,
6¾ × 5 in. (17.2 × 12.5 cm).
Galerie Bernd Klüser, Munich.

323. *Untitled.* 1988.
Black ballpoint on reinforced paper,
6¾ × 5 in. (17.2 × 12.5 cm).
Galerie Bernd Klüser, Munich.

324. *Untitled.* 1988.
Blue ballpoint on brown paper,
9 × 6¼ in. (22.6 × 16 cm).
Galerie Bernd Klüser, Munich.

325. *Untitled.* 1988.
Black ballpoint on yellow paper,
6⅝ × 8⅞ in. (16.9 × 22.5 cm).
Galerie Bernd Klüser, Munich.

326. *Untitled.* 1988.
Blue ballpoint on brown paper,
7½ × 8¾ in. (19.3 × 22.3 cm).
Galerie Bernd Klüser, Munich.

327. *Untitled.* 1988.
Black ballpoint on squared paper,
6 × 4 in. (15.2 × 10.4 cm).
Galerie Bernd Klüser, Munich.

328. *Untitled.* 1988.
Black ballpoint on squared paper,
6 × 4 in. (15.2 × 10.4 cm).
Galerie Bernd Klüser, Munich.

329. *Untitled.* 1988.
Black ballpoint on squared paper,
7¼ × 5¾ in. (18.4 × 14.8 cm).
Galerie Bernd Klüser, Munich.

330. *Untitled.* 1988.
Black ballpoint on squared paper,
4 × 6 in. (10.4 × 15.2 cm).
Galerie Bernd Klüser, Munich.

331. *Untitled.* 1988.
Black ballpoint on squared paper,
6 × 4 in. (15.2 × 10.4 cm).
Galerie Bernd Klüser, Munich.

332. *Untitled.* 1988.
Black ballpoint on squared paper,
4 × 6 in. (10.4 × 15.2 cm).
Galerie Bernd Klüser, Munich.

333. *Untitled.* 1988.
Blue and black ballpoints on
squared paper,
4 × 6 in. (10.4 × 15.2 cm).
Galerie Bernd Klüser, Munich.

334. *Untitled.* 1988.
Black ballpoint on reinforced paper,
5⅛ × 8⅞ in. (13.2 × 22.5 cm).
Galerie Bernd Klüser, Munich.

1989

335. *Untitled, no. 5.* 1989.
Pencil and ink on paper,
6¾ × 4¾ in. (17 × 12 cm).
Akira Ikeda Gallery, Tokyo.

336. *Untitled, no. 16.* 1989.
Pencil and ink on paper,
5⅞ × 8¼ in. (15 × 21 cm).
Akira Ikeda Gallery, Tokyo.

337. *Untitled, no. 19*. 1989.
Pencil and ink on paper,
3⅜ × 5 in. (8.5 × 12.8 cm).
Akira Ikeda Gallery, Tokyo.

338. *Untitled, no. 4*. 1989.
Pencil and ink on paper,
7 × 7⅞ in. (17.8 × 20 cm).
Akira Ikeda Gallery, Tokyo.

339. *Untitled, no. 2*. 1989.
Ink on paper,
7¼ × 5½ in. (18.5 × 14 cm).
Akira Ikeda Gallery, Tokyo.

340. *Untitled, no. 18*. 1989.
Ink on paper,
4 × 4 in. (10.3 × 10.3 cm).
Akira Ikeda Gallery, Tokyo.

341. *Untitled*. 1989.
Pencil on paper,
12⅞ × 19⅝ in. (32.7 × 50 cm).
Chantal Crousel Collection, Paris.

342. *Ombra vede*. 1989.
(The shadow sees)
Pencil on paper,
9⅞ × 6¾ in. (25 × 17.5 cm).
Galeria Joan Prats, Barcelona.

343. *Untitled*. 1989.
Ballpoint on paper,
7 × 9⅝ in. (18 × 24.4 cm).
Galeria Joan Prats, Barcelona.

344. *Untitled*. 1989.
Pencil on paper,
6¾ × 9⅞ in. (17.5 × 25 cm).
Galeria Joan Prats, Barcelona.

345. *Untitled*. 1989.
Pencil and marker on paper,
9½ × 6⅝ in. (24 × 16.8 cm).
Galeria Joan Prats, Barcelona.

346. *Untitled*. 1989.
Ballpoint on paper,
7½ × 5 in. (18.9 × 12.6 cm).
Galeria Joan Prats, Barcelona.

347. *Untitled*. 1989.
Ballpoint, marker and pencil on paper,
5⅞ × 8¼ in. (15 × 20.9 cm).
Galeria Joan Prats, Barcelona.

348. *Untitled*. 1989.
Ballpoint, marker and pencil on paper,
5⅝ × 8¼ in. (14.4 × 20.9 cm).
Galeria Joan Prats, Barcelona.

349. *Untitled*. 1989.
Pencil, India ink and collage on canvas,
6½ × 9¼ in. (16.6 × 23.6 cm).
Galeria Joan Prats, Barcelona.

350. *Untitled*. 1989.
Ballpoint and pencil on paper,
6¾ × 9½ in. (17 × 24 cm).
Galeria Joan Prats, Barcelona.

351. *Untitled*. 1989.
Pencil on paper,
17 × 11½ in. (43 × 29.3 cm).
Galeria Joan Prats, Barcelona.

352. *Untitled*. 1989.
Ballpoint on paper,
6 × 4 in. (15.2 × 10.4 cm).
Galeria Joan Prats, Barcelona.

353. *Untitled*. 1989.
Ballpoint on paper,
6 × 4 in. (15.2 × 10.4 cm).
Galeria Joan Prats, Barcelona.

354. *Untitled*. 1989.
Ballpoint, pencil and collage on paper,
6 × 4 in. (15.2 × 10.4 cm).
Galeria Joan Prats, Barcelona.

355. *Untitled.* 1989.
Ballpoint on paper,
6×4 in. (15.2×10.4 cm).
Galeria Joan Prats, Barcelona.

356. *Untitled.* 1989.
Ballpoint on paper,
6×8¼ in. (15.2×21 cm).
Galeria Joan Prats, Barcelona.

357. *Untitled.* 1989.
Ballpoint on paper,
8⅝×10 in. (22×25.2 cm).
Galeria Joan Prats, Barcelona.

358. *Untitled.* 1989.
Ballpoint on paper,
8½×9⅝ in. (21.8×24.5 cm).
Galeria Joan Prats, Barcelona.

359. *Untitled.* 1989.
Pencil on paper,
17½×5¾ in. (44.5×14.5 cm).
Galeria Joan Prats, Barcelona.

360. *Untitled.* 1989.
Ballpoint on paper,
8⅝×4 in. (22×10.2 cm).
Galeria Joan Prats, Barcelona.

361. *Untitled.* 1989.
Charcoal and ballpoint on paper,
8⅝×20⅝ in. (22×52.5 cm).
Galeria Joan Prats, Barcelona.

362. *Untitled.* 1989.
Pencil and India ink on paper,
8⅝×25¼ in. (22×64 cm).
Galeria Joan Prats, Barcelona.

363. *Untitled.* 1989.
Ballpoint on paper,
6×4 in. (15.2×10.4 cm).
Galeria Joan Prats, Barcelona.

364. *Untitled.* 1989.
Ballpoint on paper,
6×4 in. (15.2×10.4 cm).
Galeria Joan Prats, Barcelona.

365. *Untitled.* 1989.
Ballpoint on paper,
4×6 in. (10.4×15.2 cm).
Galeria Joan Prats, Barcelona.

366. *Untitled.* 1989.
Pencil, gouache and marker on paper,
7×12⅞ in. (17.7×32.6 cm).
Galeria Joan Prats, Barcelona.

367. *Untitled.* 1989.
Pencil, ballpoint and marker on paper,
6⅞×9¾ in. (17.5×24.9 cm).
Galeria Joan Prats, Barcelona.

368. *Untitled.* 1989.
Pencil, ballpoint, oil and collage on paper,
7×9⅝ in. (17.9×24.6 cm).
Galeria Joan Prats, Barcelona.

369. *Untitled.* 1989.
Ballpoint on paper,
7×14⅛ in. (18×36 cm).
Galeria Joan Prats, Barcelona.

370. *Untitled.* 1989.
Engraving and latex,
11⅞×11⅞ in. (30×30 cm).
Galeria Joan Prats, Barcelona.

371. *Untitled.* 1989.
Charcoal and pencil on paper, with mirror,
18¼×18¼ in. (46.5×46.5 cm).
Galeria Joan Prats, Barcelona.

372. *Untitled.* 1989.
Charcoal and pencil on paper,
18½×18½ in. (47×47 cm).
Galeria Joan Prats, Barcelona.

373. *Untitled.* 1989.
Charcoal and pencil on paper,
18⅛×17¾ in. (46×45 cm.)
Galeria Joan Prats, Barcelona.

374. *Untitled*. 1989.
Charcoal and pencil on paper, with mirror,
18½ × 18¼ in. (47 × 46 cm).
Galeria Joan Prats, Barcelona.

375. *Untitled*. 1989.
Collage, charcoal and pencil on paper,
18⅛ × 18⅛ in. (46 × 46 cm.)
Galeria Joan Prats, Barcelona.

376. *Untitled*. 1989.
Pencil, charcoal and ballpoint on paper,
18½ × 18½ in. (47 × 47 cm).
Galeria Joan Prats, Barcelona.

377. *Untitled*. 1989.
Charcoal and pencil on paper,
18¼ × 18¼ in. (46.5 × 46.5 cm).
Galeria Joan Prats, Barcelona.

BIOGRAPHY

Enzo Cucchi was born on November 14, 1949 in Morro d'Alba, near Ancona. He lives and works in Rome and Ancona.

SELECT BIBLIOGRAPHY

TEXTS BY ENZO CUCCHI

Il veleno è stato sollevato e trasportato! Macerate: La Nuovo Foglia Editrice, 1977.

"Disegno finto," in the catalogue for the "Enzo Cucchi" exhibition. Galleria de Crescenzo, Rome, 1978.

Tre o quattro artisti secchi. Modena: Emilio Mazzoli Editore, 1978.

Canzone. Modena: Emilio Mazzoli Editore, 1979.

"Die Häuser füllen sich alle bis auf halbe Höhe," in the catalogue for the "Sieben junge Künstler aus Italien" exhibition. Kunsthalle, Basilea/Museum Folkwang, Essen/Stedelijk Museum, Amsterdam, 1980-1981.

"Lettera di un disegno dal fronte," in *Enzo Cucchi: Diciannove disegni.* Modena: Emilio Mazzoli Editore, 1981.

"Di certo comunque c'è che l'immagine...," in the catalogue for the "Enzo Cucchi" exhibition. Paul Maenz Galerie, Cologne, 1981.

"Un immagine oscura," in the catalogue for the "Enzo Cucchi" exhibition. Museum Folkwang, Essen, 1982.

"Scimmia Amadriade," in *Enzo Cucchi Album: "La Scimmia."* New York: Sperone Westwater, 1983.

"Albergo," in the catalogue for the "Giulio Cesare Roma" exhibition. Stedelijk Museum Amsterdam/Kunsthalle Basilea, 1983-1984.

"Elegia," in *Parkett*, Zurich, no. 1, 1984.

"Letter from Enzo Cucchi," in *Artscribe*, No. 46 (1984).

"Italia," in the catalogue for the "Enzo Cucchi" exhibition. Anthony d'Offay, London, 1984.

"L'uomo dell'Europa," in the catalogue for the "The European Iceberg" exhibition. Art Gallery of Ontario, Toronto, 1985.

"La cerimonia delle cose = the ceremony of things," compilation of texts from *Enzo Cucchi, 1977-1985*, Mario Diacomo, ed. New York: Peter Blum Edition, 1985.

Die Zeremonie der Dinge. German translation of *La ceremonia delle cose*. Published in 1985 in Italian and English by Peter Blum Edition, New York.

"Parapetto Occidentale," in the catalogue for the "Enzo Cucchi" exhibition. Solomon R. Guggenheim Museum, New York, 1986.

Sparire: Ancona 1987. New York: Peter Blum Edition, 1987.

"Per dirigere l'arte," in the catalogue for the "Enzo Cucchi" exhibition. Centro per l'Arte Contemporanea Luigi Pecci, Museo d'Arte Contemporanea, Prato, 1989.

PUBLICATIONS ABOUT CUCCHI

CORTEZ, Diego. "Viaggio delle lune," in the catalogue for the "Enzo Cucchi" exhibition. Paul Maenz Galerie, Cologne, 1981.

CURIGER, Bice. *Looks et tenebrae: neun Monographien zu den Portfolio*. Zurich: Peter Blum Edition, 1984.

FRIEDEL, Helmut. "Testa: der Ort des Bildes," in the catalogue for the "Enzo Cucchi" exhibition. Städtische Galerie im Lenbachhaus, Munich/The Fruitmarket Gallery, Edinburgh/Musées de la Ville de Nice, Nice, 1987-1988.

KLÜSER, Bernd, ed. *Enzo Cucchi: Solchi d'Europa, 17/9/1985: AEIUO*. Munich: Galerie Bernd Klüser, 1985. Two volumes.

—. *Enzo Cucchi: Skulptur für Basel*. With a text by Jean-Christophe Ammann. Munich: Galerie Bernd Klüser, 1985.

—. *Louisiana: Enzo Cucchi: 1) 34 disegni cantano, 2) 34 disegni cantano, 3) il deserto della scultura*. With texts by Jean-Christophe Ammann, Knud W. Jensen and Bernd Klüser. Munich: Galerie Bernd Klüser, 1985. Three volumes.

LAMBARELLI, Roberto G. "Enzo Cucchi," in *Contemporary Artists*. London: Macmillan, 1983.

OLIVA, Achille Bonito. *The Italian Trans-avant-garde = la transvanguardia italiana*. Milan: Giancarlo Politi Editore, 1980.

—. *Enzo Cucchi: Roma*. Rome: Gian Enzo Sperone, 1986. Two volumes.

—. "Enzo Cucchi: Scala santa," in the catalogue for the "Ex-monastero di Santa Chiara, San Marino, 1988" exhibition. Galeria Nazionale d'Arte Moderna, San Marino, 1988.

PERUCCHI-PETRI, Ursula. "Die grossformatigen Zeichnungen von Enzo Cucchi," in the catalogue for the "Enzo Cucchi: Zeichnungen" exhibition. Kunsthaus Zürich/Groninger Museum, Groningen, 1982.

—. *Enzo Cucchi: La Disegna: Zeichnungen 1975 bis 1988*. Munich: Prestel-Verlag, 1988.

SCHELLMANN, Jörg, ed. *Enzo Cucchi: Etchings and lithographs, 1979-1985*. Munich: Edition Schellmann, 1985.

SCHULZ-HOFFMANN, Carla. "Die Malerei will die ganze Welt umfassen: Gedanken zu einigen zentralen Bildmotiven im Werk von Enzo Cucchi," in the catalogue for the "Enzo Cucchi: Guida al disegno" exhibition. Kunsthalle Bielefeld/Staatsgalerie moderner Kunst, Munich, 1987.

SCHWANDER, Martin. *Enzo Cucchi: L'ombra vede*. Paris: Chantal Crousel, 1987.

—. *Enzo Cucchi: Scultura, 1982-1988*. Munich: Zaira Mis and Bernd Klüser, Galerie Bernd Klüser, 1988.

TESTORI, Giovanni. *Enzo Cucchi: Fontana vista*. Modena: Emilio Mazzoli Editore, 1987.

VISCHER, Theodora. "Dov'è l'ingresso di un disegno?," in the catalogue for the "Enzo Cucchi: La disegna: Zeichnungen 1975 bis 1988" exhibition. Kunsthaus Zürich/Louisiana Museum Humlebaek/Kunstmuseum Düsseldorf/Haus am Waldsee Berlin, 1988-1989.

WALDMAN, Diane. "Enzo Cucchi," in the catalogue for the "Enzo Cucchi" exhibition. Solomon R. Guggenheim Museum, New York, 1986.

WEISNER, Ulrich. "Guida al disegno: die spirituelle Konzeption der poetischen Inszenierung Enzo Cucchi," in the catalogue for the "Enzo Cucchi: Guida al disegno" exhibition. Kunsthalle Bielefeld/Staatsgalerie moderner Kunst, Munich, 1987.

WILDE, E. de. "Interview mit Enzo Cucchi," in the catalogue *20 years of art collecting*. Stedelijk Museum, Amsterdam, 1984.

ONE-MAN EXHIBITIONS

1977
"Ritratto di casa, Incontri Internazionali d'Arte, Roma Montesicuro Cucchi Enzo giù," Galleria Luigi De Ambrogi, Milan.
"Mare Mediterraneo," Galleria Giuliana de Crescenzo, Rome.

1978
"Alla Iontana alla francese," Galleria Giuliana de Crescenzo, Rome.

1979
"La cavalla azzurro," Galleria Mario Diacono, Bologna.
"Sul marciapiedo, durante la festa dei cani," Galleria Tucci Rosso, Turin.
"La pianura bussa," Galleria Emilio Mazzoli, Modena.

1980
"Enzo Cucchi," Galleria Emilio Mazzoli, Modena.
"Enzo Cucchi," Galleria Mario Diacono, Bologna.
"Enzo Cucchi," Galerie Paul Maenz, Cologne.
"Uomini con una donna al tavolo," Galleria dell'Oca, Rome.

1981
"Enzo Cucchi," Sperone Westwater-Fischer Gallery, New York.
"Neue Bilder," Galerie Bruno Bischofberger, Zurich.
"Enzo Cucchi," Galleria Gian Enzo Sperone, Rome.
"Diciannove disegni," Galleria Emilio Mazzoli, Modena.
"Viaggio delle lune = Reise der Monde," Galerie Paul Maenz, Cologne/Art Project, Amsterdam.
"Enzo Cucchi," Galleria Mario Diacono, Rome.

1982
"Zeichnungen," Kunsthaus Zürich/Groninger Museum.
"Un'immagine oscura," Museum Folkwang, Essen.

1983
"Enzo Cucchi," Galerie Buchmann, St. Gallen.
"Works on paper," Galerie Schellmann Klüser, Munich.
"Giulio Cesare Roma," Stedelijk Museum Amsterdam.
"La città delle mostre," Galerie Bruno Bischofberger, Zurich.
"Enzo Cucchi," Galleria Anna d'Ascanio, Rome.

1984
"Giulio Cesare Roma," Kunsthalle Basel, Basle.
"Tetto," Galleria Mario Diacono, Rome.
"Vitebsk/Harar," Sperone Westwater Gallery, New York.
"Vitebsk/Harar," Mary Boone Gallery, New York.
"New Works," Akira Ikeda Gallery, Tokyo.
"Italia," Anthony d'Offay, London.

1985
"Arthur Rimbaud au Harar," Galerie Templon, Paris.
"Louisiana," Museum Louisiana, Humlebaek/Galerie Bernd Klüser, Munich.
"34 disegni cantano," Galerie Bernd Klüser, Munich.
"Solchi d'Europa," Galerie Bernd Klüser, Munich.
"Solchi d'Europa," Incontri Internazionali d'Arte, Rome.
"Disegni per Solchi d'Europa," Galleria Franca Mancini, Pesaro.
"Disegno vivono nella paura della terra = Zeichnungen leben in der Angst vor der Erde," Kunstmuseum Düsseldorf, Dusseldorf.

1986
"Enzo Cucchi," Centre Georges Pompidou, Paris.
"Enzo Cucchi," Solomon R. Guggenheim Museum, New York.
"Enzo Cucchi," Fundación Caja de Pensiones, Madrid/Musée d'Art Contemporain, Bordeaux.
"Enzo Cucchi," Galleria Gian Enzo Sperone, Rome.

1987
"L'elefante di Giotto," Galleria Mario Diacono, Boston.
"Enzo Cucchi," Galerie Beyler, Basilea.
"Testori," Compagnia del Disegno, Milan.
"Guida al disegno," Kunsthalle Bielefeld/Staatsgalerie moderner Kunst, Munich.
"Testa," Städtische Galerie im Lenbachaus, Munich/The Fruitmarket Gallery, Edinburgh/Musées de la Ville de Nice, Nice.
"Enzo Cucchi," Galerie Bernd Klüser, Munich.
"L'ombra vede," Galerie Crousel, Paris.
"Enzo Cucchi," Galleri Emilio Mazzoli, Modena.

1988
"Album delle grafiche con cenni storici... 1988, Cucchi fugge da Roma... era... l'epoca en... cui....," 2RC Edizioni d'Arte, Rome.
"L'italia parla agli uccelli," Marlborough Gallery, New York.
"La disegna," Kunsthaus Zürich/Museum Louisiana, Humlebaek/Kunstmuseum Düsseldorf/Haus am Waldsee, Berlin (1989).
"Scala santa," Ex monastero di Santa Chiara, San Marino.
"Uomini," Galerie Bruno Bischofberger, Zurich.
"Enzo Cucchi," Wiener Secession, Vienna.
"Enzo Cucchi," Museum Horta, Brussels.
"Enzo Cucchi," Michael Haas, Berlin.

1989
"Enzo Cucchi," Galerie Bernd Klüser, Munich.
"42 drawings," Instituto Italiano di Cultura, Toronto/Art Gallery of Windsor.
"Enzo Cucchi," Centro per l'Arte Contemporanea Luigi Pecci, Museo d'Arte Contemporanea, Prato.

PHOTOGRAPHIC CREDITS

Art Gallery of South Australia, Adelaide
131.

Akira Ikeda Gallery, Tokyo
96, 116, 118, 123, 125, 127.

Basler Versicherungsgesellschaft (Kunstsammlung), Basle
267.

Öffentiliche Kunstsammlung, Basle
29, 31, 42, 55, 95, 122.

Cosimo Bettarosa, Castagnola
3, 4.

Galerie Bruno Bischofberger, Zurich
26, 34, 36, 75, 78, 79, 117, 128, 129, 142, 223, 249, 253, 285.

Galerie Buchmann, Basle
72.

Javier Campano, Madrid
189, 190.

Compagnia del Disegno, Milan
145, 255, 256, 260-263.

Galerie Ascan Crone, Hamburg
134, 137, 247.

Fabien de Cugnac, Brussels
20, 37, 270.

Anthony d'Offay Gallery, London
130, 135, 136, 138, 187, 188, 191-195, 197, 201, 221, 240, 242.

Walter Dräyer, Zurich
12, 18, 19, 24, 28, 33, 35, 41, 51, 66, 71, 84-88, 90, 91, 93, 108, 114, 115, 121, 124, 126, 196, 232, 235, 236, 245, 265, 266, 271, 274.

Hans Gissinger, Zurich
58-65.

Foto Gross, Philipp Guyer, St. Gallen
83.

David Heald, New York
246.

Galerie Vivian Horan, New York
173.

Ralph Kleinhempel, Hamburg
76, 77, 89.

Galerie Bernd Klüser, Munich
110, 113, 147, 149-160, 163-167, 170-172, 212-215, 254, 258, 259, 268, 269, 272, 286-294.

Galerie Paul Maenz, Cologne
7, 10, 14, 25, 32, 50, 52, 54, 56, 69, 70.

Galleria Franca Mancini, Pesaro
207-210.

Franz Meyer, Zurich
11, 119, 120.

Staatliche Graphische Sammlung, Munich
107.

Solomon R. Guggenheim Museum, New York
48, 97, 98, 105, 106, 109, 112, 133, 146, 148, 161, 162, 168, 169, 174-179, 181-183, 185, 186, 204, 206, 211, 216-220, 222, 224-231, 233, 234, 237, 239, 243, 244, 248.

The Museum of Modern Art, New York
39.

Annina Nosei Gallery, New York
73.

Rheinisches Bildarchiv, Cologne
6.

Peter Schibli, Basle
250, 257, 264.

Philipp Schönborn, Munich
1, 2, 273.

Sperone Westwater, New York
99, 100, 103, 104, 202.

John Stoel, Groningen
5, 23, 82.

Dorothy Zeidman, New York
43-47, 67, 74, 80, 81, 92, 94, 139-141, 143, 144, 198, 205, 238, 241.

Zindman/Fremont, New York
99, 100, 101, 102.

J. Littkemann, Berlin
15, 16, 22, 40.

Florian Kleinefenn
341.